言い返さない日本人

装　　　幀＝斉藤　啓（ブッダプロダクションズ）
翻　　　訳＝ルーシー・ノース
編集協力＝エド・ジェイコブ, iTEP JAPAN

本書は2009年に小社から発行された『言い返さない日本人』（対訳ニッポン双書）を
加筆・修正したものです。

言い返さない日本人

海外との
究極のコミュニケーション術

新装版

TALK
BACK!

山久瀬洋二

YAMAKUSE YOJI

IBCパブリッシング

はじめに

　外国人と仕事をして、「あれっ?」と思ったことはありませんか?
　誤解される日本人、そして日本人に誤解される外国人。日本人と
出会った外国人の**本音**がここに。

　笑えるものから深刻なケースまで、いろいろな状況がありますが、
わかってしまえば、これこそ異文化コミュニケーションの醍醐味と
いう、行き違いがあちちで起こっています。

　わかりにくい日本、奇妙な日本人、腹立たしい日本人、困った日
本人、でもとっても面白く、すてきな日本人という彼らのコメント
を通して、日本人に必要とされる海外とのコミュニケーション術を
ここに紹介します。
　本書で語るのは、私が実際にコンサルタントとして接してきた96
社の国際企業に働く4千500名の外国人と日本人との**ビジネス上の
摩擦**の事例から最も頻繁におこる28ケースを抽出しました。そこに
は彼らが本音で語ってくれた、**苦しみ、切望**があります。

　すでに30年以上、私は幾度となく、外資系、日系の国際企業をた
ずね、そこに働く外国人、日本人の双方にインタビューを重ね、そ
んな誤解を分析し、コミュニケーションの改善、**生産性の向上**を目
指してきました。

　世界が日本に否応なく、押し寄せています。好き嫌いに関係なく、
海外の人が日本で、日本人が海外でビジネスを展開し、共にチーム

Preface

Has there ever been something that made you say, "What the…?" when working alongside foreigners?

Japanese get misunderstood by foreigners, and foreigners get misunderstood by Japanese. This book contains the **true feelings** of foreigners who have encountered Japanese.

There are various incidents, from the humorous to the serious, and once you understand them, you will see that these misunderstandings are caused mainly by fundamental cultural differences in communication and occur all over the place.

Through foreigners' comments about how Japan can be difficult to understand, and how the people can be strange, irritating, or troublesome—but at the same time interesting or wonderful, we'll explain the communication skills Japanese need to get along with foreigners.

This book contains 28 real examples of the most frequently occurring incidents that I have encountered while working as a consultant. I have selected all the cases from actual examples of **business-related friction** between 4500 foreigners and Japanese working at 96 international companies. They contain the real feelings that have been expressed to me about their **hardships** and **aspirations**.

Over the past 30 years I have many times had occasion to visit foreign capital ventures in Japan as well Japanese international enterprises. I have analyzed the misunderstandings from numerous interviews conducted with both the Western and the Japanese interviewees, and these are included with the aim of improving communication and **promoting productivity**.

Whether Japan likes it or not, the world is pressing in on it. And whatever the Japanese may think of the matter, foreign people are

を作って同じ目標に向けて**プロジェクトを推進**しています。

　もちろん、外国の人たちも、日本人も、心からビジネスの成功を祈って、精一杯努力します。ところが、時とともに単なる言葉のギャップでは片付けられない誤解や、摩擦、そして行き違いをお互いが体験します。目に見えないビジネス文化の違いが、双方にいろいろな**罠を仕掛けてくる**のです。お互いに熱心であればあるほど、罠は執拗に人々の足をとらえようとします。**柔軟に対応**して、そんな罠を回避し、むしろ文化の違いを活用したより強力なチームワークを創造する人たちもいます。しかし、時には相手に不信感を抱き、それが次第に無力感となってしまい、ビジネスそのものが活力を失ってしまうケースも見受けられます。

　文化の違いによる、ちょっとしたコミュニケーションの方法の違い、あるいはコンセンサスのとり方や、合意のとり方の微妙な差異が、そうした行き違いの原因になるのです。思わぬところに**落とし穴**があるのが、異文化間でのビジネスの特徴なのです。

　とはいえ、異なる文化との出会いは楽しいものです。人々の異なる行動様式や思考方法からは、その背景にある様々な歴史的事象、あるいは宗教観、時には政治や経済的な事情を垣間見ることができます。そして、それらの文化の強いところが活かされれば、単一文化のみではなしえることのできない多彩で幅の広いビジネスも展開できるのです。そして、そんなビジネスが世界に広がれば、人々の交流が広がり、国際間の理解も深まっていくはずです。

coming to Japan, and the Japanese are going to foreign countries—developing businesses, and setting up teams together and **conducting projects** toward the same aim.

Needless to say, both non-Japanese and Japanese want nothing more than for their businesses to succeed, and they do everything in their power toward this end. Inevitably, however, as time passes they experience misunderstandings, and friction arises from differences that cannot be put down to simple gaps in communication. Discrepancies in the business cultures of each country, invisible to the eye, **pose traps** that wait for both sides. The more eagerly each tries to get on with the other, the more tenacious the traps seem to be. People exist who can **respond with flexibility** and manage to avoid the traps, and who can facilitate powerful team-work using the cultural differences to mutual advantage. However, sometimes people bear a distrust for people from other cultures: and that distrust can gradually lead to a feeling of apathy, and occasionally a company can lose all its drive and energy because of this.

Cultural differences, small differences in communication methods, or subtle disparities in the ways agreements are made or consensuses reached, give rise to the disagreements that are the cause of this distrust. One of the characteristics of doing business in different cultures is that there are unexpected **snares** you can fall into.

Even so, encountering a culture entirely different from one's own can be a highly enjoyable experience. Behind the differing **modus operandi** in people's behavior, or their different thought processes, one catches glimpses of the influence of various historical phenomena, or religious views, and inevitably political and economic factors too. And if we can take advantage of the strong features of differing cultures, sometimes a truly colorful, broad-ranging business can be developed which would have been impossible from a single culture alone. Surely this is the reason for corporations to spread their wings

であればこそ、私たちは、ここに紹介する異文化が故の誤解や行き違いの実例を見つめ、それが起こる所以を理解したいものです。誤解の中には一見滑稽なものも多々あります。でも、**当事者**はみな真剣です。待ったなしのビジネスの場において、私たちがいかに柔軟に対応し、誤解のメカニズムを解明しながら、異なった価値観やコミュニケーションの方法に心を開いていけるか。この課題はグローバライゼーションの波にもまれる日本そのものの課題といっても、差し支えないのではないでしょうか。

山久瀬　洋二

around the world! When this type of truly cross-cultural business does evolve on a global basis, true communication and exchange will take place, and international understanding can deepen.

It is precisely for this reason that I would like everyone to look at the situations included in this book, at the differences and misunderstandings that arise out of two different cultures coming to grips in order to understand the reasons why they arise in the first place. At first glance, many of the misunderstandings seem even comical, but the **people involved** are all deadly serious. In the business world, where few second attempts are allowed, how to deal with matters flexibly, and throw light on the stumbling blocks that trigger misunderstandings? How to open our hearts to different value systems and different communication styles from our own? Such questions should concern the whole of Japan, buffeted as it is by the waves of globalization.

Yamakuse Yoji

目 次

はじめに 4

序章　異文化の罠がもたらす思わぬ誤解とは 16

第1ラウンド
あいまいだよ、日本人 39

事例1 日本の皆さん、悲しいよ。
なぜ本当の気持ちを語ってくれないのですか。 40

事例2 ねえねえ、日本の皆さん、あなた方が何をしてほしいか
わからないのです！ 48

事例3 あのさあ。横ばかり向いてないで、
ちゃんと自分で意見を言ってよ!! 54

事例4 おい、日本人さん、
フィードバックをくださいな!! 62

事例5 日本人はなぜもっと自分をアピールしてくれないの？....68

事例6 日本人のほほえみって不気味だよ。
本心がわからないんだよ。 74

事例7 Business is business、
あなたたちわかってるの？ 80

事例8 おいおい、日本人さん、
そんなに緊張しないでよ。 88

CONTENTS

Preface 5

Introduction 17
What are the unforeseen misunderstandings brought
created by differences in cultures?

ROUND 1

The Japanese Are so Vague 39

Case 1 Japanese people, it's so sad. Why don't you say what
you really think?.. 41

Case 2 Hey, Japanese people, I have no idea
what you really want! 49

Case 3 Listen. Don't always be looking at each other.
Tell me your opinion directly!! 55

Case 4 Hey, Mr. Japanese, would you *please* give us
some feedback?.. 63

Case 5 Why don't Japanese people bring up
their strengths more?... 69

Case 6 The faint smiles on Japanese people's faces are creepy.
I really don't understand them... 75

Case 7 Business is business.
Do you understand that?.. 81

Case 8 Hey there, Japanese people, don't be so nervous. 89

第2ラウンド

言っていることがわからないよ、
日本人 95

事例9 そんなことを聞いているんじゃないよ。
ちゃんと質問に答えてくれ！ 96

事例10 プレゼンテーションの勉強をすべきだよ、
日本人は。 102

事例11 日本人は、言葉足らずであいまいだよ。 108

事例12 ねえ日本人、ベネフィットがなけりゃ
やる気なくすよ。 114

事例13 ブレインストーミングなんだから
日本人も参加してよ!! 120

事例14 どうして日本人は感情や感傷で
ビジネスをすすめるの？ 126

事例15 日本人は本気で謝ってるの？
謝るなら結果をだしてよ！ 134

第3ラウンド

外国人と一緒に働けない日本人 141

事例16 日本人の上司にお願い。
僕のことを評価してよ。頼むから。 142

事例17 それは個人の領域。
日本人はなんで首をつっこんでくるんですか？ 150

事例18 僕も仲間に入れてよ。どうして日本人だけで
いつもかたまってしまうの？ 158

ROUND 2

I Don't Understand What You're Saying, Japanese People 95

Case 9 That isn't what I asked you.
Answer my question first! 97

Case 10 Japanese people really have to bone up on
their presentation skills. 103

Case 11 Japanese aren't explicit enough—they leave
everything vague. 109

Case 12 Um, Mr. Japanese, if there's no benefit,
we'll lose our motivation. 115

Case 13 It's brainstorming, so Japanese people have to
participate too! 121

Case 14 Why do Japanese do business in such an emotional,
sentimental way? 127

Case 15 Are the Japanese really sincere when they apologize?
If you're really sorry, do something about it! 135

ROUND 3

The Problems Japanese Have Working with Foreigners 141

Case 16 Japanese boss, *please* give me some praise. 143

Case 17 That's a private matter. Why do Japanese poke their
noses into everything? 151

Case 18 Let me into your group. Why do Japanese always
stick together only with other Japanese? 159

事例19 日本人はなんであんな人を採用しようと
するのだろうか? 166

事例20 チームワークとグループ活動を混同する日本人 172

事例21 過去は過去。未来志向でいこうよ、日本人! 178

事例22 責任領域がはっきりしない日本企業では、
自分を伸ばせないよ!! 188

事例23 日本の人事制度は差別の温床。
とても耐えられなかったよ。 194

第4ラウンド

グローバルになれない日本人 203

事例24 日本の特殊性だって?!
もう耳にタコができたよ。 204

事例25 なんで日本人だけを信用するんだい?
僕たちはいつもかやの外…… 210

事例26 日本人よ、どこまで任せてくれるの?
しっかりとした方針を決めてほしい。 218

事例27 日本人よ、グローバルだよ、グローバル!!
あなたたちは孤立したいのかい?................................226

事例28 頑張ってシナジーを構築しよう!!....................................232

Case 19 Why do the Japanese hire that kind of person?........167

Case 20 The Japanese confuse "teamwork" with
"group activities" 173

Case 21 The past is the past. Look to the future,
Japanese people..179

Case 22 I can't get ahead at a Japanese company where areas
of responsibility are so fuzzy!!..189

Case 23 The Japanese personnel system is a breeding ground
for discrimination. I couldn't stand it..195

Japanese Problems with Being "Global" 203

Case 24 I'm tired of hearing about Japanese uniqueness. 205

Case 25 Why do Japanese people only trust other Japanese?
We're always regarded as outsiders. 211

Case 26 Mr. Japanese! How much are you going to leave up to
us? Decide on a firm policy! 219

Case 27 Mr. Japanese! The world is globalizing. Globalizing!!
Do you want to isolate yourselves?...227

Case 28 Create synergy by working together! 233

序章

異文化の罠がもたらす
思わぬ誤解とは

コミュニケーションスタイルの違いが思わぬ落し穴に

　海外の人とビジネスをする上で、常に落とし穴となるのが、文化の違いによる誤解に気づかずに相手を評価してしまうことです。

　いうまでもなく、自らの価値観や常識は、生まれ育った国や地域によって異なります。問題は、そうした価値観や常識に支えられた行動のみがお互いの目や耳を通して、情報として個々人にインプットされてしまうことなのです。

　そしてインプットされた情報は、それぞれの異なった常識や価値観によって判断され相手への評価へとつながってしまいます。その結果思わぬ誤解がおき、さらにその誤解は気づかれないまま、ビジネスや国際交渉に様々な影響を与えてしまうのです。

　それは、ちょうど氷山の上の部分だけが海面上にあって、私たちにはその部分しか見えていないことを考えればよくわかります。この氷山の概念は1980年代頃からビジネスでのコミュニケーションのメカニズムを解析するメタファー（例示）として多くの学者が使用し、研修などでも披露されてきました。

Introduction

What are the unforeseen misunderstandings brought created by differences in cultures?

Differences in communication styles become unexpected pitfalls

In doing business with people from other countries, there is a constant risk that results from making judgments about the other party without being aware of misunderstandings that result from a difference in cultures.

Needless to say, a person's sense of values and common sense varies depending on the country and region where that person was born and raised. The problem is that the information regarding an individual is taken in through the eyes and ears of another person who is entirely supported by the sense of values and the common sense that is part of the observing individual.

The information that is taken in is assessed by that person's unique common sense and sense of values, and that in turn affects the person's evaluation of the other party. As a result, unexpected misunderstanding occurs and, without those involved having any awareness that this has happened, it has diverse impacts on business and international negotiations.

It is helpful to think of this in terms of the metaphorical iceberg, where all we can see is the top of the iceberg which rises above the level of the ocean. This iceberg metaphor has been in use since the 1980s among academics and in-service training coaches as a way of describing the mechanism of communication in business.

つまり、私たちが長年それぞれの文化に基づく教育や社会環境の影響を受けて培ってきた価値観や宗教観、さらには物事の判断基準は氷山の下の部分、すなわち他の人には見えない水面下に隠れているのです。

　そして、そうした価値観などによって表現される言動は、水面の上に目に見える行動や言葉となってあらわれます。もっというならば、私たちはそうした行動をみて、そして言葉を聞いて、自分が水面下にもっている価値観などでその言動を判断したり評価したりしていることになるのです。

　実際、多国間や異文化間ではその価値観や宗教観などが大きく異なるために、しばしば相手のコミュニケーションのスタイルに対してマイナスの評価をしたり、相手の発するサインを誤解して受け取ったりしてしまうのです。

　この異文化のメカニズムを知っておくことは、海外に駐在したり、海外からの訪問者と仕事を円滑に進めたりする上で極めて重要です。さらに、海外の企業や個人とプロジェクトを進行させてゆくときに、無駄な誤解による時間やコストの浪費を大幅に削減できるのです。

　逆にいうならば、もし相手のコミュニケーションスタイルを理解し、その原因となる行動様式を支える価値観への柔軟性を持つことができれば、ビジネスでの生産性の向上が促進されることになります。

　例えば、日本人が善意をもって相手に語りかけたことが、相手からみるとモチベーションの低下につながることもあり得るのです。そのことを事前にわかっていれば、海外の支社などでの離職率を下げ、相手とプロダクティブな交流が促進されるため、お互いの知識やアイデア、さらに情報をより効果的に活用し合えるようになるのです。

　逆に、そうした理解の欠如がもたらす損失は思いのほか大きなものとなることはここで特に強調したいと思います。

That is, our sense of values and our religious views, as well as standards for evaluating things, have been cultivated over long periods of time under the influence of our respective educational and social environments and they constitute the lower part of the iceberg. To wit, it is below the surface where other people can't see it.

The speech and behavior that is expressed as a result of our own sense of values comes out in the visible part of the iceberg: our words and deeds. To be more explicit, we can see the behavior and hear the words of the other person and judge and evaluate those elements based on the values that we maintain below our own water line.

In dealings between different cultures, due to the fact that there is a great disparity between them, the sense of values and religious views of one culture may lead one to a negative evaluation of the other party's communication style and may cause one to misinterpret the signals given off by the other party.

Having an understanding of this difference in cultural mechanisms is extremely important when one is stationed abroad or when one wants to smoothly carry on business with visitors from overseas. With this understanding, in the process of carrying out projects with businesses and individuals overseas, one can substantially reduce wasted time and energy that might result from unnecessary misunderstandings.

Conversely, if one can comprehend the other party's communication style and maintain flexibility toward the values that support the style of behavior that underlies it, it will promote an improvement in business productivity.

For example, a Japanese may approach a person with good will, but the other party may take it in a way that reduces his or her motivation. If one is aware that this could be an issue, it would reduce the rate of job turnover in overseas branch companies. By improving productive interaction with others, there could be more mutual sharing of ideas and knowledge, as well as effective practical application of knowledge.

What I would especially like to emphasize is that, in the reverse case, a lack of such understanding may bring about unexpected losses.

日米間のギャップを見つける３つのステートメント

　ここで次の文章を読んでください。

　**「多くの人が参加する会議の場で、自分と異なった意見であれば、た
とえ上司の発言であっても、異議を堂々と表明することに躊躇しない」**

　この文章についてその通りだと思い、自分はそのように行動するとい
う人は5点をつけるとします。逆に、それは無理だし、なかなかそうは
できないと思う人は1点をつけます。そして状況によって異なるがどち
らかといえばその通りだと思う人は4点、その逆は2点、どっちとも決
めかねる人は3点をつけてみます。そこで、日本人とアメリカ人を例に
とって、この文章への反応を予測してみましょう。実際多くの人が予想
する通り、日本人には1点から3点までの人が多く、アメリカ人は4点
から5点までの人が多くいます。

　つまり、日本人には「遠慮」「相手の顔を立てる」「立場を考える」「和を
保つ」などといった常識や価値観があり、組織の中にいる場合、ここに
記した文章のように行動することに躊躇してしまうのです。

　ところが、アメリカ人はというと、ビジネス上の議論は立場や上下関
係を超えて堂々と平等にたたかわせても構わないという倫理観がありま
す。ですから、上司の前でも異なった意見があればそれを率直に表明し
ます。その背景には「平等」「ディベートをよしとする文化」「ビジネス上
の意見を個人攻撃と分けて捉える」といった常識や基準があるからです。

　ということは、もし国際会議に出席し、関係者への「遠慮」から自分
の主張を表明せずに黙っていたり、曖昧な表現に終始したりすると、ア
メリカ側からみればその人への評価は最悪で、無視されても文句は言え
なくなります。

Three statements that help uncover gaps between Japan and America

Please read the following statement.

"During a meeting with a large number of participants, if I disagreed with someone's opinion—even one voiced by my superior—I would not hesitate to openly express my opinion."

On a scale of 1 to 5, someone who fully agrees and would act accordingly would give this a 5. In reverse, someone who thinks that would be impossible and would not be able to act accordingly would give this a 1. Someone who believes that it would depend on the situation, but would basically agree with the statement would give this a 4. In reverse, a person who would hesitate but might, depending on the situation, speak up would give this a 2. A person who could not decide either way would give this a 3. Let's now take the example of how Japanese and Americans react to this statement. As most people would expect, most Japanese respond to this statement with a 1, 2, or 3, while most Americans give this a 4 or 5.

In other words, for Japanese, common sense and their sense of values include restraint, making others look good, taking one's status into account, and maintaining harmony in a group. Within an organization, they would hesitate to act in accord with the perspective in the statement above.

On the contrary, Americans follow a code of conduct that sees no problem in participation in business discussions without self-restraint or consideration of rank and permits open discussion of issues as equals. Therefore, even in the presence of a superior, one can candidly express a contrasting opinion. In the background of this stance is the common view and standard which is based on equality, a culture that approves of debate, and an expression of opinions in business that is not considered an attack on the person.

In sum, consider the case of a person attending an international meeting who remains silent as a result of "self-restraint" in the presence of others, refraining from stating an opinion, and instead simply offers rather ambiguous comments from start to finish. From the perspective

逆に、日本人は遠慮なく自分の主張だけをしてくるアメリカ人を横柄で高圧的だと評価するかもしれません。

　面白いのが次の文章への評価です。

「仕事の進め方に関して、上司に最初から最後まで詳しく指導してほしいとは思わない」

という文書に、日本人は上司にしっかり把握し指導してもらいたいと思い、1点から2点をつける人が多かったことに対して、アメリカ人のほとんどが5点をつけ、上司は部下の仕事のやり方を細かく把握する必要はないと思っていることがわかったことです。

　日本人がそう答えた背景には、プロセスや型を大切にする価値観があり、それを教え学ぶところに上下関係があるという常識があるからでしょう。それに対してアメリカ人は「自由」「独立心」「個人主義」といった価値観がビジネスでのコミュニケーションのあり方にも影響を与えていることがみえてきます。

　そして、この回答の結果からいえることは、日本人がアメリカ人を、そしてアメリカ人が日本人をマネージする方法に、それぞれの価値観に基づく違いがあって、そのためにお互いの信頼関係にも影響を与えかねないという深刻な警告につながっているのです。つまり、日本人はプロセスをより重んじて上司と部下との人間関係の構築に注力します。一方、アメリカ人は、プロセスは部下の判断に任せ、結果に対してフィードバックを重ねることで部下の能力を開発しようするのです。 このように、部下への指導方法には日米で大きな違いがあるのです。

　こうした傾向がより鮮明に出ているのが、

of attending Americans, he will be given the worst possible evaluation, but he will not be able to complain if he is totally ignored.

In reverse, Japanese will regard an American who asserts his own position without taking others into consideration as arrogant and high-handed.

The responses to the next statement are intriguing.

"In regard to the completion of a job, it is not desirable to have detailed guidance from one's superior from start to finish."

In response to this statement, out of a desire to have a superior thoroughly understand and offer guidance in one's work, most Japanese gave this a 1 or a 2. In contrast, almost all of the Americans gave this a 5. From this we can see that Americans don't believe that it is necessary for a superior to maintain a detailed grasp of how a subordinate is carrying out a job.

In the background of the Japanese response is a set of values that places emphasis on process and form, and this is inculcated by the accepted practice of maintaining relations between higher and lower ranks. In contrast, the sense of values held by Americans emphasizes freedom, independent spirit, and individualism, and this has an impact on the way in which communication occurs in in the workplace.

From the results of these responses, we can see that there is a difference in the way Japanese manage Americans and the way Americans manage Japanese. These methods are based on entirely different value systems. This should serve as a clear warning that the difference may have an impact on relationships of trust. That is to say, Japanese place emphasis on the process and concentrate on building human connections between superiors and subordinates. Meanwhile, Americans leave the process to the discretion of the subordinate, and by repeated feedback regarding the results, they develop the subordinate's abilities. Hence, there is a major difference between Japanese and Americans regarding the method of instructing subordinates.

This tendency is made even more distinct in the responses to the following statement.

「上司から注意を受けても、もし自分が正しいと思ったら、自分がなぜそうしたか理由を説明する。また、その注意の内容に納得できなければ、特に詫びたりもしない」

という文章にアメリカ人のほとんどが5点満点で同意したのです。

顧客対応のしかたにも日米間の違いが現れてきます。アメリカ人の価値観の根本にある「平等」という意識からみて、たとえ顧客であってもまずはお詫びという行為はありえません。上司が注意したときでも、時には「あなたの指示が曖昧だったからですよ」などと部下が反論し、指摘をすることすらあるのです。

この行為をみて、「立場」とか「謙遜」や「謙虚」といった価値観を持つ日本人には、「彼らは注意すればすぐに言い訳をする」と映ってしまうのです。

そして、同じようなギャップがみられたのが、次の文章への感想です。

「プロジェクトは、過去の検証をすることにこだわるより、未来志向でこれからの目標に重きをおくべきだ」

確かに日本人は完璧な準備とコンセンサスがなければ前に進もうとはしません。そのため過去の失敗にばかりこだわって、そこを検証しない限り次の行動には移りにくいのです。過去を重んじる文化背景を持つ人々の典型が日本人のビジネス観に現れてくるようです。

一方、アメリカ人はほとんどの人がこのステートメントに賛同し5点をつけます。そんなアメリカ人の言動をみて、日本人は「なんと無責任な」と愚痴を言い、アメリカ人はいつまでも過去の細かいことにこだわる日本人にうんざりするのです。

"Even if a superior offers advice on how to do something, if I believe that my way is correct, I would explain why I did it that way. If I can't be convinced by the content of the advice, I would feel no reason to offer an apology."

In response to this statement almost all of the Americans gave it a 5.

This is also a difference between Japanese and Americans in dealing with customers. Seen from the basic importance of equality in the American value system, even when responding to a customer, the first action taken is not to offer an apology. Even when a superior makes a suggestion or criticism, a subordinate might disagree and, on occasion, even indicate that the instructions he or she received were not clear.

In the eyes of Japanese, who place emphasis on rank, modesty, and humility as elements of their value system, such behavior by Americans would be lead the Japanese to say, "When I caution them about something, they immediately make excuses for themselves."

The same kind of gap can be seen in responses to the following statement.

"In a project, rather than focusing on a review of past experience, one should be more oriented toward future goals."

There's little doubt that Japanese will not move forward without complete preparation and consensus. As a result, they are obsessed with past failures and until they have examined those completely, they would find it difficult to move forward. A representative example of people with a cultural background emphasizing the past can be found in Japanese business.

In contrast, almost all of the American respondents supported the statement, rating it as a 5. Looking at the words and behavior of Americans, Japanese grumble about how irresponsible Americans are. Meanwhile, Americans become fed up with the Japanese obsession with fine details from the past.

異文化摩擦を予防する2つの方法

　ここでこれらの3つのステートメントを含む6つの文章を表にしてみました。皆さんで、それらに対して1から5までの数値をつけてみてください。数値が高ければ良いことで、数値が低ければ悪いことというわけでは全くありません。これは単に文化による判断基準の違いを明確に理解するためのツールに過ぎないのです。

　そして、もしあなたが海外の人と一緒に働いている場合、このチャートを海外の人にも試してもらうのも一案です。ここには英文のチャートも用意しています。

　そして、あなたの数値と相手の数値との開きが大きいところが、お互いのコミュニケーション文化の違いから起こる誤解のリスクが介在する箇所となります。

　さらに深く分析をするために、数値の記入が終わった段階で自らの数値を足してみます。6点から30点の合計点がでてくるはずです。

	← そうは思わない　その通りだ→				
1. 会議やミーティングの場で、たとえ上司や他の人の意見と違っていても、上下関係を気にせずに自由に意見を言うべきだ。	1	2	3	4	5
2. 人と話している時にわからないことがあれば、調べたり後から説明を求めたりするのではなく、状況に関わらずその場で説明を求めるべきだ。	1	2	3	4	5
3. 上司は部下の仕事の進め方を、プロセスも含め最初から最後まで詳しくしっかりと指導する必要はない。	1	2	3	4	5
4. 部下や同僚、上司との職場を離れた交流はそれほど必要とは思わない。また、業務の状況のいかんを問わず、自分の都合で必要であれば休暇を取ることに抵抗はない。	1	2	3	4	5
5. プロジェクトでは過去の検証をしっかりしようとこだわるより、未来志向で、これからの目標に重きを置くべきだ。	1	2	3	4	5
6. 上司から注意を受けても、相手が納得するまで、自分がどうしてそうしたのかを説明するべきだ。	1	2	3	4	5

Two methods of preventing intercultural friction

The following is a table that lists six sentences including the three statements that we have discussed. Please give a numerical value from 1 to 5 to each. Whether the value is high or low is neither good nor bad. This is only intended as a tool for understanding clearly the difference in standards for judgment according to culture.

If at some point you work with someone from abroad, you might consider having that person try this, too. That is why the English version is included.

If there is a wide disparity between the numerical value you assign and that which the other person assigns, it is one occasion where there is a risk of misunderstanding that may result from a clash between communication cultures.

For further analysis, once you have assigned a numerical value to all of the items, add the numbers together, for each person. Your total should be between 6 and 30.

	← Less likely			More likely →	
1. In conferences and meetings, you should feel free to express your opinion—even if it is different from your superior's or other opinions—without considering the hierarchy.	1	2	3	4	5
2. If you are talking to someone and you don't understand something, you should ask for a clarification on the spot, regardless of the situation, rather than look something up or ask for clarification later.	1	2	3	4	5
3. A superior should not have to completely grasp all details of his or her subordinate's work from start to finish, including the process.	1	2	3	4	5
4. I don't believe that I need to interact socially (e.g., go out for dinner or drinks) with my subordinates, colleagues, or superiors. Also, I am not afraid to take leave if necessary for my own reasons, regardless of the work situation.	1	2	3	4	5
5. Projects should focus on future goals rather than inspection of the past and precedents.	1	2	3	4	5
6. When you have a critical feedback from your boss, you do not hesitate to explain your reason if his or her feed back is not suitable.	1	2	3	4	5

過去の調査では、日本人の平均点は13点、アメリカ人は26点となっています。もちろん、個性や年齢によってその点数が上下することもあるでしょう。しかし、この結果をみてそこに自分自身の英語力を加味してみると、相手との誤解が発生する確率の高さに危機感を覚えてしまうかもしれません。

　こうした誤解を防ぐためにも、お互いに結果を見せ合って、そのギャップのある部分について文化背景の違いを説明し、それを埋めてゆくノウハウを話し合うことが大切です。

　このギャップを認識するために、ここにもう一つチャートを用意しました。

　この円グラフに注目してください。そこには14の項目が示されています。14の項目はそれぞれ矢印によってお互いにペアを構成しています。

　例えば、Individual はGroupと矢印で結ばれていることがわかると思います。

　これは、ビジネスでのコミュニケーション文化の違いをお互いに理解するためのもう一つの指標となります。

　そこで、この一つ一つのペアについて解説してみましょう。

According to past surveys, Japanese average 13 points in total, while Americans average 26. Of course, these figures are higher or lower depending on the individual and the person's age. However, if you look at these results and add in the issue of your own English proficiency, you may become more aware of the danger implied by the probability of a gap between you and the other person.

In an effort to prevent misunderstandings, you might show one another your respective results, and explain the cultural background of the items where gaps exist. It's important to discuss the differences and the skills that you might employ to overcome those differences.

Here is one more chart that helps one become aware of these disparities. Please look at the following pie chart. It shows 14 items, each of which is connected to by a pair of arrows.

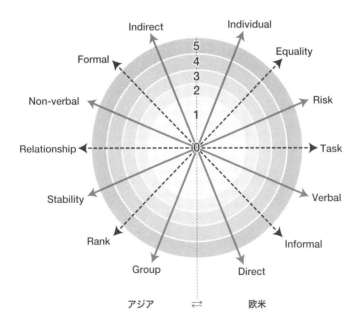

1) Individual ⇄ Group

　自らの考えや思いを堂々と表明し、自ら積極的にリーダーシップをとることを前向きに支持する環境がIndividual（個人）的環境となります。それに対して仲間や所属するグループのコンセンサスや和を最初に意識した上で自分の行動を決めがちな環境におかれている人はGroup（集団）的環境にいるということになります。

2) Equality ⇄ Rank

　仕事上の上下関係はあっても人としては平等で、上司でも先輩の前でも比較的カジュアルに自分の意見や意思を表明しやすい環境がEquality（平等）な環境です。それに対して組織の縦社会がより大きな意味をもち、そのヒエラルキーに対して敬意を払いながら行動する環境はRank（地位）を重んずる環境となります。

3) Risk ⇄ Stability

　ビジネス上、リスクをかけることに比較的ハードルが低く、個人としてもより積極的に自分の能力をアピールしプレゼンテーションできる環境がRisk（リスク）をとる文化で、それに対して前例や過去の状況を重んじ、より慎重に物事に対処しようとする文化をStability（安定）を求めるビジネス文化であるということができます。

4) Task ⇄ Relationship

　仕事をまず進め、業務についての決裁も比較的早めに行い、その上で次第にお互いの関係性や立ち位置を意識し調整するビジネス文化をTask（業務行動）を重視するビジネス文化とします。一方、自らが置かれている状況や人間関係を考えながら、慎重に根回しやお互いを知るためのコミュニケーションを行った上で決裁をし、物事を進めていこうとする文化をRelationship（関係性）を重視したビジネス文化であるとします。

1) Individual ⇄ Group

An environment that actively encourages a person to frankly express his own thoughts and feelings and is positive in supporting people to actively take leadership is an "Individual" environment. In comparison, an environment which tends to seek consensus and harmony among the companions or group to which one belongs before taking action is a "Group" environment.

2) Equality ⇄ Rank

Even though there are vertical relations in the workplace, the individuals are equals. An environment in which one can, with comparative casualness, easily express one's own ideas and intentions to even one's superior and seniors is an environment of "Equality." In contrast, an environment in which a vertically structured organization plays a larger role, and in which one acts in accord with the requirements of the hierarchy is an environment that values "Rank."

3) Risk ⇄ Stability

Where taking risk in business faces a comparatively low hurdle and allows individuals to actively demonstrate abilities and make presentations, the environment is a "Risk" culture. In contrast, where a business stresses precedent and past situations and is cautious in making business decisions, the environment seeks to maintain a culture of "Stability."

4) Task ⇄ Relationship

Where one proceeds with work first, operational approval is carried out relatively quickly, and relations between people and awareness of positions evolve gradually, the business has a "Task" oriented culture. In contrast, where one is particularly conscious of the conditions and personal relations in one's surroundings, cautiously carrying out prior consultations and communications so people will know one another, the business has a "Relationship" oriented culture.

5）Verbal ⇄ Non-verbal

　自らの考えを言葉でしっかりと説明し、その言葉の内容を相手の意思として理解しビジネスを進める環境がVerbal（言語）に頼ったビジネス環境です。それに対して言葉の背景や無言のニュアンスなどでやんわりと意思疎通を図り合いビジネスを進めようとする環境がNon-verbal（非言語）的なコミュニケーションスタイルを重んじる文化となります。

6）Informal ⇄ Formal

　基本的に誰に対しても気遣うことなくフランクに接することのできるビジネス環境をInformal（カジュアル）な文化とします。それに対して、相手によって姿勢やものの言い方を変え、時には立場や地位によって発言方法などにも一定の常識が課せられるビジネス文化がFormal（フォーマル）な文化であるとします。

7）Direct ⇄ Indirect

　どんどん率直にものを言い、直裁にお互いにフィードバックをし合える環境をDirect（直裁）なビジネスコミュニケーション文化がある環境であるとし、それに対して相手の立場や面子などを意識し、時には持って回ったコミュニケーションをしたり、人を介してフィードバックを行ったりするビジネス文化をIndirect（間接的）なビジネス文化と定義します。

　多くの場合、日本を含むアジアはチャートの左側、そして右側が欧米型のビジネス文化に当てはまります。その度合いが1であれば少なく、5であれば頻度や状況がよりその概念に当てはまるわけです。

　これを見ながら、日本人がどのような場合に相手に誤解を与えてしまうかを考えてみます。

5) Verbal ⇌ Non-verbal

A culture where one can firmly express one's thoughts and the respective parties can move forward on the basis of a common understanding is a business with a "Verbal" environment. In contrast, in an environment where business is carried out on the basis of attempts at a flexible mutual understanding dependent on the context of words and unspoken nuances, the emphasis is on "Non-verbal" communication.

6) Informal ⇌ Formal

A business environment in which one can basically deal frankly with anyone without apprehensions is one with an "Informal" culture. In comparison, a business environment in which one changes one's attitude and manner of speaking depending on who one is addressing and where a set understanding of how one should express oneself depends on status and situation has a "Formal" culture.

7) Direct ⇌ Indirect

A business environment in which one does not need to hesitate to speak to others in plain language with directness in exchanging feedback is one which has a "Direct" culture. In contrast, an environment in which one is conscious of the other's position and face-saving, where communication is at times roundabout, and feedback is conveyed through intermediaries has an "Indirect" culture.

In most cases, the business cultures of Asia, including Japan, belong on the left side of the chart and Western business cultures belong on the right side. If the rating is a 1, that is small. If the rating is a 5, then the frequency and conditions are applicable.

Looking at this, let's consider what kinds of situations exist in which a Japanese might cause misunderstanding among non-Japanese.

例えば、上司が同席し、その上司がより日本型のビジネス文化の染まった人であった場合、あなたはたとえ英語が堪能であっても、上司が相手の指摘や意見、あるいは相談に対して曖昧な対応をしていることに気づいた場合、それをはっきりと指摘しづらいのではないでしょうか。そして、ただ黙ってメモをとることに徹してしまい、心の中で、「会議のあとで彼らと非公式に調整しよう」と考えるかもしれません。

　これがRankを重んじIndirectなコミュニケーション文化をもつ日本では当たり前の行動とされがちです。

　しかし、上司の前でも自分をアピールし、どんどん率直な意思表示をすることをよしとする欧米の人たちは、そうしたあなたの行動が理解できず、信頼できない人だと誤解するかもしれないのです。
　こうした違いを端的にあらわしたのがこの円グラフなのです。

　異なる国や地域での価値観や常識を映像にすることは不可能です。

　それは、相手にとっても同様なことで、それがそれぞれの国民へのステレオタイプやイメージへとつながります。「アメリカ人は」とか「中国人は」という相手を評価する感想が生まれるとき、その感想を持つ背景に自らの価値観が反映されていることを知っておくべきです。そして海外の人も「日本人は」というイメージを持っているはずです。

　実は、世界での交渉ごとでの不調や決裂、さらには妥結後に不協和音などがおきる原因のほとんどは言葉の問題ではなく、こうした見えない文化背景の罠に起因するのです。そして、このことは21世紀になった現在でも充分に分析されていない課題なのです。人はほんの数分で相手

For example, imagine that you and your superior are meeting a client. Your superior is deeply imbued with typical Japanese business culture. Imagine also that you are proficient in English. Now, imagine that you become aware that your superior is responding to the other party's points, opinions, and ideas in an ambiguous manner. Would you not feel it awkward to point this out to your superior? If so, you might simply withdraw from participation in the conversation and devote yourself to taking notes, thinking to yourself that after the meeting you will need to make some informal adjustments to what was discussed in the actual meeting.

According to the "Indirect" business culture in Japan, where "Rank" is emphasized, this would be a perfectly normal course of action.

However, from the perspective of Americans, who accept making oneself understood and express themselves straightforwardly without hesitation, your actions would be hard to understand and you would be seen as an untrustworthy individual.

This difference is clearly illustrated in the pie chart.

It is impossible to generate a visual image of the disparities that exist between different countries or regions in terms of their value systems or what is taken for granted as common sense.

The same thing is true for everyone, and this leads to the creation of stereotypes and images of people from different societies. When one forms impressions of other people that are value judgments such as "Americans are…" or "Chinese are…" one must remember that the base for such judgments is one's own value system. And people overseas undoubtedly have an image that leads them to comment "Japanese are…".

In actual fact, around the world where negotiations stall or collapse entirely or when a settlement is reached only to be followed by discord, the main cause is not simply a language problem but a problem resulting from this invisible cultural background. Even now, at the beginning of the 21st century, this issue has not been sufficiently taken into account. People evaluate others within just a few minutes

を評価し、その人柄まで判断してしまいます。それは国と国の間でも同様なのです。

　ただ、ここで強調したいことがあります。

　それは、最初に指摘したように、もしこの異文化での摩擦を解明し、それを乗り越えることができた組織は、より広範で多様なアイデアや能力を世界中から結集できる強いチームへと成長できるということです。それは単一文化だけに支えられる企業ではあり得ない強い発酵力を醸成し、上面からも効率の上からも相乗効果が期待できるようになるはずです。

　次の章からは28の典型的なビジネスの摩擦のケースを紹介し、そこで発生した誤解のメカニズムとその解決方法を具体的に分析してみたいと思います。

and make judgments about their character on that basis. The same is true of nations.

I would like to make one point clear.

As was pointed out at the beginning, if an organization is able to unravel the conflict that results from differences in culture and to overcome that conflict, it will be able to grow into a strong team capable of bringing together even more extensive, diverse ideas and capabilities from around the world. That organization could be expected to do something no company supported by a mono-culture could possibly do: develop a strong synergy yielding benefits in both sales and efficiency.

In what follows I will examine 28 cases of typical business conflict and the mechanisms of the misunderstandings that led to them. I will then analyze them in detail to show methods for solving such conflicts.

あいまいだよ、
日本人

ROUND **1**

The Japanese Are so Vague

日本の皆さん、悲しいよ。
なぜ本当の気持ちを語ってくれないのですか。

> 日本に行って、お客さんと会うと歓迎してくれるよね。でも、帰国した後でその時には聞いていなかった苦情が矢のように飛んでくる。いったいどうなってるの？　お願いだ。僕の目の前で本当のことを言ってよ。

外国人の不満　私は、日本人に向けて衣類を輸出しているイタリア人です。私はいつも日本側のパートナーから、日本の得意先はとても品質にうるさくて、今のような品質管理だと**満足しない**し、実際にいろいろなクレームがお客さんからきているぞと言われている。本当にうるさいよ。

　そこで、日本への出張のときに得意先を回って現状を把握しようとするけれど、得意先と会っているときにはそんな問題提起は全くないんだ。それどころか、我々のサービスに感謝しているような感じで、なごやかな雰囲気でミーティングを終えて、あとはお酒と日本食の楽しいディナー。時差ぼけの僕にはちょっと大変だけどね。

　ところが、帰国するとまたその得意先からクレームの嵐がきていると、日本サイドからガミガミと文句が届く。いったい、どうなってるの？日本の相棒が、お客に過敏に反応しすぎているのかなあ？だって、あのお客さん、いつもにこにこして、その上おいしいお酒だけじゃなく、お土産までくれたんだよ。

日本人の反論　あのさ、ちょっと日本に来たからって、なんでも理解

Japanese people, it's so sad.
Why don't you say what you really think?

> When we go to Japan and meet our clients, they give us a warm welcome, but then after we get back home we get a barrage of complaints and dissatisfactions that were never voiced at the time. Please. Tell it to my face.

Foreigner's grievance: I'm from Italy, and I export clothes to Japan. I'm always told by my partners on the Japanese side that clients in Japan are **fussy about** the quality of the goods, that they're **dissatisfied with** our present quality control, and that in fact they themselves are getting all sorts of complaints from their Japanese customers. They never shut up.

So, during our business trips to Japan, we make a point of going to visit our clients to try to get a grasp of the actual state of affairs. But when we meet with our clients, no mention at all is made of such problems—on the contrary, they give the impression of being pleased and grateful for our services. The meeting always ends in a very harmonious mood, and afterwards we go out for an enjoyable Japanese dinner and drink sake. It's a little difficult for me because I have jetlag.

But as soon as we get back to my country, here come the complaints again thick and fast from the Japanese side, that they're overwhelmed with complaints about the goods from our clients. What in the world is going on? Is it just that our Japanese partners are over-reacting to what the customers say? I mean, this customer always has a big smile on his face, and he gives us not just good sake, but souvenirs as well.

Japanese retort: Hey, it's no good when you just arrive in Japan

できたような気になられても困るんだよ。あなた方はいったいどれだけ得意先と一緒に時間を過ごしていると思っているんだい。たった1週間だよ。今回の出張だって。しかも大急ぎで得意先を回って。

日本人は、**人間関係を構築する**中で徐々に意見を交換しはじめる。伝統的な会社ではなおさらなんだ。そんな場合、ひょっこり外国から訪ねていっても、当たり障りのない応対しかしてくれないに決まっているじゃないの。

まだ十分に人間関係が構築されていないから、得意先は日本に来た外国のお客さんとして、あなた方をもてなすけど、彼らの本音やクレームは人間関係がすでに構築されている信頼のおける日本人のセールスの人に話すわけ。そして得意先はそのセールスの人を通して、間接的にあなた方にメッセージが伝わることを期待しているんだよ。それがどうしてわからないの?!

分析

多くの欧米から来た人は、ビジネス上のミーティングでは常に**具体的に**討議する課題があって、課題をその打ち合わせの中で解決したいというビジネス文化を持っています。

だから彼らにとって、日本流の間接的な、持って回ったやり方を理解することは非常に困難です。「問題があれば、ミーティングで直接表明して欲しい。そのためにわざわざ日本に来ているのだから」と思ってしまうのです。

しかし、本人の前で直接文句を言うのではなく、間接的にメッセージを伝えることは、日本では失礼なことではありません。むしろそれは摩擦を起こすことなく、穏便に問題を解決しようという日本流のコミュニケーション術といえますね。実はこの、人を

thinking you know everything. How much time did you spend with the client? You only spend one week here. Like this last trip. You just rush around visiting clients.

Japanese people exchange opinions only very cautiously, in the course of **building up relationships** with each other. This is all the more true in a traditional company. If you just pop in for a quick visit from abroad and then go away again, of course, what more can you hope for than superficial, neutral responses?

And since they don't have a proper relationship with you, the Japanese clients direct their claims to your Japanese partners who deal with sales, with whom they have built up a relationship and whom they can therefore trust. What they hope is that the message will get through to the American side indirectly, through these Japanese sales people. Why aren't you a bit more aware of these subtle aspects of doing business in Japan?

Analysis

In Western countries, particularly in the U.S., corporate culture expects business meetings to involve discussions of **concrete** problems and themes which have to be solved during the meetings.

As far as foreigners are concerned, the Japanese way of doing things, which is so long-winded and time-consuming, is extraordinarily tiresome. They tend to think, "If there's a problem, why don't they come out with it in the meeting? This is, after all, why we've **taken the trouble** to come to Japan."

In Japan, however, voicing a complaint directly in front of the person involved tends to be avoided, and getting a message through to him or her indirectly, through another person, is not considered rude. Rather, it's a way to avoid friction and to solve the problem in a harmonious way. This is a particularly Japanese style of communication

介した間接的なコミュニケーションが多くの外国人を戸惑わせてしまうのです。

外国からの訪問者に一言前もって伝えてはどうでしょう。もし得意先と会う機会があるのであれば、その前に十分に情報を収集し、得意先の前では何か問題があったならば、まず謝りましょう（なぜ謝ることが必要なのかは、第2ラウンドの事例15を参照してください）と。しかし、そのときお客さんは「いえいえ、ご心配なく。大丈夫ですよ」と言うかもしれませんね。それは、まだあなたが十分にお客さんと人間関係を構築していないことからくる得意先の**外交辞令**なんだと、海外の人にわかりやすく説明してはどうですか。

日本側のパートナーは、得意先に対して外国からの相棒の紹介をちゃんとしておきましょう。そして、たった一度の訪問で人間関係が構築できると期待しないことを相棒に伝え、大きなビジネスに結びつけるには、何度も、たとえ解決すべき課題がなくても得意先のところに挨拶に行くというスタンスが必要だとわかってもらいましょう。何よりも大切なことは同僚の日本人を介して、すでに良い人間関係を構築している人を食事などに招待し、楽しい時を共に過ごすこと。そうした交流を通して、だんだんと相手は問題点や課題を直接、語ってくれるようになるはずです。人間関係が構築されれば、今度はこちら側からも相手に対して間接的に重要なメッセージを送れるようになるはずですね。

実は、得意先から問題を提起され、クレームを受けている日本人も、得意先の本音が海外のパートナーに伝わらないために、パートナーが本気になって問題を解決してくれないと悩んでいるはずです。この悩みを解決できるのは、海外の相棒に日本でのビジネスの進め方を理解してもらう以外に方法はないはずです。**地道な努力**の末に築かれた人間関係は、強固なもの。そんな土台があ

and these relationships using intermediaries can be bewildering to non-Japanese.

How about giving a little warning to foreign visitors in advance? If they do get the chance to meet with a Japanese client, they should first gather as much information as possible so that when they meet with them, they can apologize about there having been a problem (on the reasons for apology, see Round 2. Case 15). At this point, the client will probably brush the apology aside and say, "Oh, don't worry, everything is fine." This is nothing but **superficial politeness**, and derives from the fact that no proper relationship has been built up between them. So how about explaining this to the foreigners in an easy to understand way?

The Japanese partner should formally introduce the foreign partner to the Japanese clients. Next, they shouldn't expect that a proper relationship will develop between them and the clients with just one meeting. Even if no problem exists that needs a solution, they should be prepared to pay a visit to the clients' office several times over. And probably most important, they should invite people with whom they do already have a good relationship out to a meal or some such thing, with the help of Japanese colleagues, so that they can spend a relaxing time together. It's through this kind of exchange and socializing that the other party will gradually feel able to tell them of problems and issues that have to be dealt with. And through the connections that are built up in this way, they will be able to get important messages across to the other party too.

In fact, the Japanese staff, who are on the receiving end of the claims and complaints, and being told about the problems by Japanese clients, are probably themselves concerned that the foreign partner's company won't be able to deal with the problems seriously precisely because they haven't been informed about how the clients truly feel. In order to alleviate these worries, there is no other way than for the Japanese partner to make the foreign partner aware of the Japanese way of doing business. Relationships that have been built up with **solid effort** are very secure. Inform the foreign partner in advance

ってはじめて大きな仕事を一緒にできるということを前向きに相棒に伝えましょう。特に人間関係を重視する日本のビジネス環境では、一度構築されたビジネスの関係は簡単には崩れないのですから。

　そうです。日本では仕事を通して人間関係を構築するのではなく、まずよりよい人間関係があって、本格的なビジネスに移行できるのです。これは、まずストレートにビジネスを進めることから始めようとする欧米と日本とのビジネスに関する基本的なスタンスの違いです。このことを考えながら、ぜひ日本側のパートナーと共に、得意先との交流について作戦を練って欲しいものですね。

ソリューション

❶ 得意先との人間関係の構築こそが、得意先の本音を聞き出す近道であるということを、まず外国人のパートナーに説明しよう。

❷ 外国人を責めるのではなく、より強固な関係を築き得意先に喜ばれるには、何をしたらいいかを考えながら、外国人と一緒に悩み、得意先に対応するスタンスをもとう。

❸ 得意先との密な交流にできるだけ外国からのパートナーにも参加してもらい、無理のない範囲で夕食やゴルフなどの付き合いも促進し、そこでの本音の会話ができるよう、コーディネートしよう。

that once such a foundation has been laid, you will be able to accomplish big things together. Especially in the Japanese business world, which lays great emphasis on such things, once a relationship has been built up, it will be very difficult for it to break down completely.

That's right: in Japan, you don't build up a relationship through working together—rather, it's only when you have built up a good relationship that you can then move on to do proper business. This is a fundamental difference in the attitudes to business between the countries of Europe and the United States, where people get right down to business immediately, and Japan. So do please bear this in mind, and with the help of your partners on the Japanese side, try to refine your strategies regarding your interaction with your clients in Japan.

Solution

❶ First, explain to your foreign partners that the quickest shortcut to hearing what your clients really think is by building a strong personal relationship with them.

❷ Rather than criticizing foreigners partners, please the customer by using the approach of thinking with your foreign partner about what can be done, worrying together, and responding to the customer in order to build a stronger relationship.

❸ Get your partner involved as much as possible in close exchanges with the customer by arranging dinners and golf games, etc., where the partners will have a chance to hear the customers' real feelings.

ねえねえ、日本の皆さん、あなた方が何を してほしいかわからないのです！

ときどき日本人が何を求めているのかわからなくなるんです。それでいて、後になって、ぐずぐずと文句を言い出すからたまらない。言いたいことははっきりと言ってよ‼

外国人の不満　私は日本人からの依頼でアメリカで商品の買い付けをしているんです。でも、ときどき商品の在庫が無くなっていたり、日本からの支払いが遅れたりして商品を思うように届けられないことがあるんです。そのことを説明すると、そのときは「オーケー。わかりました」って日本人は言うんだけど、しばらくして「あれはどうなった？ なぜその後の状況を教えてくれないんだ」って、さんざん文句を言ってくるんです。

　私は日本人がいったい何を望んでいるのかわからなくなる。彼らのリクエストはいつもあいまい。それでいて、満足できないと、一方的にこちらを責めてくる。ときどきそんな日本人にうんざりしてしまいます。

日本人の反論　我々からみて、あなたがたは無責任なんですよ。あなたがたは私たちのニーズを理解しようとしない。商品を発注してそれが在庫切れだったのはわかる。でも、それならいつその商品が入手できるのかちゃんと調べて、我々に知らせてくださいよ。

　それだけじゃない。もっと我々に働きかけて、その商品の代わりにこうした商品があるけどそれを代替にできないかとか、他の業者をあたってみようかとか、しかるべき対応をしないじゃないですか。

Hey, Japanese people, I have no idea what you really want!

Sometimes Japanese don't make clear what it is that they really expect or want you to do. And then, later on, what do you know, they start to grumble and complain. Say what you want!

Foreigner's grievance: I make purchases of goods in the United States for Japanese people in Japan. But occasionally stocks run out, or payments from Japan are late and the goods don't arrive according to plan. When I explain that, the response I get from the Japanese at the time is usually, "No problem, we understand." But then, after a while, I start getting all sorts of complaints, like "Did you do anything after that? Why didn't you give us any more information about things afterwards?"

I have no idea what it is that Japanese people actually want. The requests they make of you are so vague, and yet, if they're not satisfied, they start blaming us as if it's all our fault. Sometimes those guys make me so **fed up**.

Japanese retort: From our point of view, you are not doing your job with the right degree of responsibility. You're not making any effort to understand what our needs really are. We understand if stocks are out when we place an order, but surely you should then make all the more effort to try to find out when exactly you'll be able to lay in more goods, and to inform us.

And that's not all. Surely the obvious way of handling the situation would be to try to persuade us to buy something else that might be just as good as the item we couldn't get, or to offer to try somewhere else to find the same item.

仕事に**本気**で取り組んでいないんだよ。そんなことでよくビジネスができるもんだと思うよ。そもそも、日本でのニーズをしっかり勉強しようという姿勢が足りないと思うんだ。我々は取引先なんだから、取引先が満足するように、勉強するのは当然のことだと思うんですがね。

分析

　日本人から見て、**かゆいところに手がとどかない海外のサービス**にうんざりするケースはよくあることです。しかし、意外にもそこには文化の違いからくる誤解が介在するケースが多くあります。それはニーズに対してどのように対応するかという考え方についての違いなのです。

　アメリカ人を例にとれば、アメリカ人はニーズのある側が、そのニーズをしっかりと相手に伝えることがビジネス上のコミュニケーションの第一歩であると考えます。それに対して、日本人は相手のニーズを察して行動することをよしとするのです。

　例えば、日本人が話し相手に「お腹空いていない?」と聞いた場合、相手の空腹を尋ねているケースだけでなく、尋ねている本人がお腹が空いていて、暗にそのことを伝えようとしていることがありますね。そのとき、聞き手は相手のニーズを察して、「何を食べようか?」と質問を返すわけです。それに対して、アメリカ人の場合は、自分にニーズがなければ「別にお腹は空いてないよ。大丈夫」と答えてしまいかねません。話を切り出した方が「お腹が空いてきたけど、君はどう? 何か食べにいかない?」とはっきり自らのニーズを表明して、はじめて相手とのコミュニケーションが成立するのです。

　したがって、この外国人の言い分には彼なりに一理あるわけで

You're not **serious about** business. Do you think that attitude will help do good business? You're not doing enough to meet the needs of your Japanese clients from the start. We are the clients, so we would have thought it should be your job to find out what will satisfy us.

Analysis

Japanese people often get fed up with the service they get from foreign companies, which often seems rather **half-hearted**. But actually, in most cases, the reason that problems arise has more to do with cultural differences than anything else. The difference here lies in what is considered the appropriate response for a company to make to customers' needs.

To take America as an example: to an American, it's the responsibility of the side with the needs to let the other side know exactly what those needs consist of—this is the first step in communication in the corporate workplace. However, to a Japanese, it is considered a good thing to try to surmise what the other person might want, and then to act accordingly.

For example, when a Japanese says to someone, "Aren't you hungry?" it is often the case that he won't just be inquiring about the state of someone's appetite, but will be trying to get across a subtle message that he himself would like to eat. In such a situation, the other person surmises the questioner's need and answers with something like, "What shall we eat?" To an American, the response to such a question would probably be, "No, I'm not, I'm fine"—and the real message would only get across if the first person said, "I'm feeling hungry, how about you? Shall we go eat something?"

So, there is a kind of logic to what the foreigner is complaining about here. When stocks of goods run out, he expects the Japanese

す。日本側がその商品が在庫切れの場合、何をしてほしいか、自らのニーズを明確に伝えてはじめて相手も対応をするわけです。

　　異民族が混在しているために、相手のニーズを察することが難しかった欧米の人々と、長い間、同じ言語と同じ風俗習慣を共有していたために、相手のニーズに先回りしてしまう日本人との発想法の違いがこうした誤解の原因となるのです。このことを日本側はちゃんと理解して、あいまいに自らのニーズを伝えないよう心がけたいものです。

　　そして、外国人のあなたは、そうした日本人の発想法を理解して、常に相手が表明している意見や言葉がどういった気持ちに根ざしているのか、相手の気持ちに立って考えてみる必要があるのです。すなわち、ただ日本人の言うことをうのみにせず、相手の気持を**推測**して相手におだやかに同じ質問を返してみるのも大切なコミュニケーションの方法なのです。

ソリューション

❶ 欧米の人と話をするときは、含蓄をもたず、あうんの呼吸に頼らずに自分のニーズをはっきりと表明しよう。お腹がすいたよ、何か食べないかと。

❷ わかってもらったはずなのにという誤解を避けるには、話し合った直後にメールなど、文章で確認を。時には事前にこちらのニーズを文章にして渡しながら話し合いを進めよう。

❸ 大事なことは、ニーズがある場合、ニーズのある方がそれをしっかりと伝える責任があるというビジネス文化を理解することだ。

side to tell him what they want him to do, to make clear what their own needs are—and then he will take the appropriate measures in response.

The cause of this kind of misunderstanding surely lies in the differences of thinking arising from the fact that in Europe and America all sorts of people of **different ethnicity** lived in the same area, making it difficult to guess how others might feel and what they might want. But in Japan, people have shared the same language and customs for a long time, so that they are used to thinking about other people's needs first. The Japanese side should understand and make allowances for this, and make efforts not to be vague in getting their needs across.

And Westerners, you too should make allowances for the Japanese way of thinking. You should also try to see things from your Japanese partner's point of view, and make an effort to consider what feelings lie beneath the opinions and words he or she might be expressing. In short, don't take the things he or she says simply at face value: an important way of communicating is to try to **gauge** your partner's feelings, and to gently reply to his questions with the same sort of questions of your own.

Solution

❶ When speaking with Westerners, explain what you need clearly without implying things or relying on unspoken communication. Tell them that you are hungry and suggest eating.

❷ In order to avoid confusion about matters you thought were understood, do things like sending emails to confirm them in writing immediately after discussions. In some instances, it is recommended that you put down your needs on paper ahead of time when having discussions.

❸ It is important to understand that in business culture, when people have needs, they have a responsibility to communicate them.

あのさあ。横ばかり向いてないで、ちゃんと自分で意見を言ってよ!!

日本人はなぜ率直に自分の意見を言わないの? 自分が意見を言うかわりに、横を向いて「君どう思う」なんて言いながら、他人を介して意見を伝えたりして。ちょっと卑怯だと思うんですけど。

外国人の不満 私はロンドンで出版社に勤務していて、商談で定期的に日本に来ています。その商談で、時々理解できないことが起きるんです。

よく日本人は**はっきりとノーと言わない**というけれど、それくらいのことなら**我慢できる**わ。でも、最も嫌なのは、そのあいまいな答え方ではなくて、自分は何も言わずに、私を無視するように、隣の人に話しかけて、その人を通して間接的に意見を伝えようとするそのやり方なの。

この前商談で、私が「田中さん、この企画についてどう思いますか」と尋ねたところ、田中さんは横にいた部下の斎藤さんの方を見て、「どう思うかね」と聞くんです。すると斎藤さんが、「ちょっと難しいんじゃないですか」って言うと、田中さんは「そうだよな。うーん」と言って黙っている。結局、明解な答えをもらえないわけです。そしてうやむやになるか、時には斎藤さんを通して今は困難だというような、あいまいな連絡がきたりする。なぜ、田中さんは自分の意思を直接私に言わないのでしょうか?

こんなこともありました。私が日本での慣習を知らずに、ある日本人に失礼なことをしたことがありました。ところが、後になって、別の人からその人が腹を立てていることを聞いたんです。なぜ、直

Listen. Don't always be looking at each other. Tell me your opinion directly!!

> Why don't the Japanese just come out with their own opinions frankly? Instead of coming out with what they themselves think, they look at each other and say, "What do you think?" and get others to voice their opinions for them. It seems kind of cowardly.

Foreigner's grievance: I work for a publishing company in London and regularly come to Japan for business meetings. There are sometimes things I can't understand at the meetings.

You often hear that Japanese can never say "no" **outright**, and I can **put up with** that. But the thing I dislike the most, even more than their way of only giving vague answers, is the way they start talking to the person beside them, ignoring me as if I wasn't there. Then they try to get their opinion across through the other people instead of voicing it for themselves.

In a meeting the other day, for example, when Mr. Tanaka was asked what he thought of a certain plan, he looked at his junior, Mr. Saito, who was at his side, and asked: "What do you think?" Mr. Saito then said, "I think it might be somewhat difficult," and Mr. Tanaka followed with "Hmm, yes," and then fell silent. In the end, I couldn't get a clear answer. All I got were either non-committal replies, or vague messages that came through Mr. Saito that it was "probably impossible right now." Why doesn't Mr. Tanaka just tell me himself what he thinks?

Oh yes, and then you get this kind of thing happening. In my ignorance of Japanese customs, I did something that offended a Japanese. But I heard later from a third party that the man was really furious with me. I couldn't understand why he hadn't told me himself—it

接私に言ってくれなかったのかと思うとがっかりしました。日本人は自分の気持ちや意見を率直に人に伝えない、卑怯なところがありますね。

もしかしたら日本では女性の地位が低いから、私が女性なので適当にあしらっているのかしら。そうだとしたら、日本って相変わらず体質の古い国なのね。

日本人の反論 何でも白か黒かをはっきりさせたがる外国人には閉口しますよ。時にはグレーのままこちらの意思を伝えたいことだってあるんだから。だって、もし私が面と向かって、「あなたのここは問題です」なんて言えば、角が立つじゃないですか。

私は相手の気持ちを考えて、あえて**婉曲**に表現しているのに、そんなこともわかってくれないんだから、嫌になります。こちらが気を遣えば遣うほど、性急に白黒つけたがるんですよ。時にはたたみかけるように答えを求めてくることすらあるんです。すると、こちらはますます相手に気を遣って、あいまいになったりする。だから、他人を介してこちらの意見を伝えようとしたりするんです。

そう、こちらは結構、繊細に対応しているんですよ。それなのに、彼らは相手の気持ちを考えて、こちらの言いたいことを汲み取っていこうとはしないんですかね? それをしないというならば、こちらはもっと強く、はっきりとものを言うべきなのかな? 日本人はそんなコミュニケーションのやり方には慣れていないんですが……。

分析

日本と欧米、特にアメリカとのコミュニケーションで最も際立った違いが、自らの意見をいかに相手に伝えるかという意思の伝

made me so disappointed. There's something cowardly about the way Japanese people don't tell you their opinions or feelings frankly, which really bothers me.

Maybe it's because women have a low position in Japanese society, so he doesn't take me seriously. If that's how it is, Japan is an old-fashioned country that hasn't changed with the times.

Japanese retort: Why is it that Westerners always have to have everything up front, in black and white? There are times, you know, when one wants to get something across vaguely, in gray. I mean, if I just said something like this straight to his face, "There's such and such a thing wrong about you," he'd just get mad, wouldn't he?

I hate the way, even though I'm doing my best to express myself **indirectly** so as not to hurt his feelings, he shows no appreciation of that. The more care I take in expressing myself, the more vehemently he seems to demand that everything be stated in black and white. There are times when he fires a volley of questions at me, demanding immediate answers. Then I end up trying all the more not to offend him, and become more and more ambiguous. That's why finally I have to resort to a third person to get my opinion across.

That's right, I for one am doing my best to deal with the guy sensitively. Does this mean foreigners never think of the other person's feelings, that they never make any attempt to try to surmise what we on this side might be trying to say underneath the words? If they don't, then isn't it up to us to try and be more explicit and clear in our statements? Being so direct is not something that most Japanese are used to in their way of communication.

Analysis

Here we can see one of the most conspicuous differences in communication between Japan and Western countries—particularly the United

達方法に見受けられます。

　伝統的に欧米の人は、個人とビジネス上の感情とを分けて対応する傾向にあります。ビジネス上の意見の交換は、別に相手個人に対してなされているのではなく、相手とのビジネス上の事柄に対してなされているとみるのが彼らの特徴でしょう。彼らは、たとえはっきりとノーと言っても、それは個人に対して発言しているのではなく、単なるビジネス上のやりとりと割り切るのです。

　日本人の場合、得てしてビジネス上の**意見交換**は、そのまま個人のコミュニケーションのあり方とダブってしまいます。だから、日本人は相手に対してはっきりと拒絶したり、相手に注意をしたりすると、その人が傷ついたり、気分を害するのではと危惧するのです。したがって、日本では**第三者を介して**、クッションを置きながら意見を交換したり、あえてあいまいな表現をして、相手に**それとなく**意思を伝達しようとするのです。

　これは元々、**身分制度**のあった日本で、立場の上の人に直截にものを言うことがタブーとされていた古い伝統に起因するのかもしれません。あいまいで微妙な表現の中から真実を感知し合うことは、日本人が**封建時代**の昔から行ってきた伝統的なコミュニケーション・スタイルと言えましょう。

　それに対して、欧米の多くの人は、本人に直接、明快なコミュニケーションをすることが、相手を尊重したマナーであると考えるために、日本流の**持って回った**意思の伝達方法に苛立ったり、失望したりするのです。

　特に身分制度が存在せず、常に対等な人格として相手と対応してきたアメリカ人などの場合は、相手に明解な意見を述べないことは、相手を信頼していない危険なサインということになるわけです。

States—and that is in the methodology surrounding transmission of one's own thoughts and opinions to another person.

Traditionally, Americans have tended to deal with matters making a division between their feelings as individuals and their emotions on the job. It's characteristic of Americans to regard the exchange of opinions in business matters as not carried out with the other person as an individual, but in the context of one's relationship with the other person in matters of business. So even if an American says "no" outright, straight and simple, this is not a personal refusal: it is seen simply as part of an exchange on a business level.

In the case of Japanese, however, an **exchange of opinions** in business matters more often than not takes on the same significance as the way individuals communicate on a personal level. This is why Japanese become wary of simply saying no outright, or pointing out faults in the other person—they worry that they'll hurt the other people's feelings or offend them. Accordingly, in Japan it's most common for people to exchange opinions **through a third party**, using him or her for "cushioning" effect, trying **in a roundabout way** to get their opinion across by using vague expressions.

This practice probably derives from much older traditions, from the days when Japan had a **hierarchical society**, and it was strictly forbidden to voice any desire or opinion in a direct way to any person of a higher status. One could perhaps say that grasping the central kernel of truth that lies within vague, subtly expressed words is a traditional style of communication that Japanese people have been using for many hundreds of years, since **feudal times**.

Most Westerners, however, think that it is a mark of good manners and respect to the other person to say things directly and clearly. They get irritated and disappointed at Japanese communication methods, which are so **circumlocutory**.

Particularly for Americans, who come from a country where a hierarchical class system never existed, and who deal with others always as individuals on an equal basis, to never make your opinion clear to the other person is taken as a sign that you feel danger, that you don't trust the other person.

　ここではイギリス人の女性のコメントを紹介していますが、得てしてこうした誤解は、女性として差別されているのではというような、日本人の意図を超えた誤解にも発展しかねません。特に、面と向かった対話の場合、日本人は相手の目を見ずに、アイコンタクトを弱くして**会話を進め**がちなため、さらなる誤解が生まれてしまうのです。

　日本人はあいまいだとよく言われますが、そこにはこうしたコミュニケーション・スタイルの差異があるわけです。したがって日本人と商談などをして、相手の意見をしっかりと聞き出すためには、両者の間に立ってクッションの役割を担うコーディネーターを置くと効果があります。コーディネーターは日本人の微妙なニュアンスを理解し、伝達するのみならず、時にはコーディネーターを介して日本側が自らの意思を伝えてくることもあるからです。

　持って回ったような、一見堂々としていないように見えるやり方が、実は日本人にとっては最も安心できる、そしてマナーに適ったメッセージの伝達方法だということを、外国人も知っておくといいかもしれません。

ソリューション

❶ いつでも相手の目を見て、相手に直接話しかける対応を。日本人同士で打ち合わせるときは、その旨をちゃんと相手（外国人）に伝えよう。

❷ ビジネスはビジネス。だから、むしろはっきりとイエスかノーかを伝えた方が、相手にとってはありがたいのだ。

❸ 異文化経験のない上司や関係者と、海外からの訪問者とをうまく調整できるコーディネーターのロールも見直してみよう。

We have included the comments of a British woman here, but the likely misunderstanding is that she thinks she is being discriminated against because she is a woman, which is not what Japanese people intend. Especially in face-to-face discussions, Japanese don't look others in the eye and **carry on the conversation** with little eye contact, which can lead to serious misunderstandings.

It is often said that the Japanese are inscrutable; but this derives from these differences in communication style. Hence, in business talks with Japanese, if you want to get a clear picture of the opinions of your Japanese partners, a good way of doing this is to have someone stand in between you and the other side as a coordinator, who will take on the role of "cushion" between the two parties. That person will be able to understand and transmit the subtle nuances expressed by the Japanese, and the Japanese side will also on occasion transmit their opinions across to you of their own accord through that person.

It would be as well to know that this method, which appears circumlocutory and repetitive, is in fact the one that makes Japanese people feel most secure and is thought to accord with manners. It would be very helpful for foreigners to be aware of this way of conveying one's message.

Solution

❶ Always maintain eye contact and respond directly to the person you are talking to. If you are going to start discussing something with other Japanese, tell the foreigner about it before you start talking.

❷ Business is business, so people hope the people they are talking to will say yes or no directly.

❸ Review your role as coordinator so you can successfully conciliate between superiors and others who have little experience with cultural differences and your visitors from abroad.

おい、日本人さん、
フィードバックをくださいな!!

日本人は我々のやったことをありがたいと思っているんだろうか? 彼らから我々についての意見や評価を聞くことはほとんどないので不安になるんだ。

外国人の不満　僕は日本人と仕事をしていてときどき不安になるんです。いったい彼らは僕のしていることに満足しているんでしょうか? 彼らはこちらのやったことをほとんど評価してくれない。本当にありがたく思っているのか、それともどこかを改善してほしいのかさっぱりわかりません。

　僕は自分のキャリアのことを考えます。これだけしっかりと仕事をしていながら、それをちゃんと評価してくれないなら、それは自分のキャリアのためにも、日本人との仕事を辞めなければと思ってしまいます。

　そんな日本人でもときどき「ありがとう」って言ってくれることはあるんです。だけど、いったい何についてありがたく思っているのかが伝わってきません。どうなっているんでしょうか。

日本人の反論　日本ではいちいち相手に自分の気持ちを伝えなくたって、長い間培われた人間関係で自ずと相手がどのように思っているかわかるもんなんです。それをいちいち相手に「よかったねえ。もっと頑張ろうね」とか「君は本当に仕事ができるね。特にこの書類のまとめかたはすばらしかったよ」なんて伝えようものなら、なんか相手を子供扱いしているかのように思われてしまいますよ。

Hey, Mr. Japanese, would you *please* give us some feedback?

Do the Japanese feel any appreciation at all for the jobs we do for them? We think not, because we hardly get any praise or evaluations at all.

Foreigner's grievance: Working with Japanese, I sometimes start to get really worried: are they actually satisfied with the work I do for them? They hardly ever tell you if what you did was any good. I have no idea whether they are pleased with it, or if there is something that they want me to do better—or what.

I have my career to think about. If I'm trying my best to carry out my job well, and they're not going to think I'm any good, I end up wondering whether it wouldn't be better as far as my career is concerned to just stop working with them.

Sometimes a Japanese will say "Thanks." But even then, he or she doesn't actually make it clear what it is I am being thanked for. What is going on here?

Japanese retort: In Japan, in any relationship that has been built up over time, it's going to be obvious what each person thinks of the other, even if neither is putting his or her thoughts into words all the time. Come on—if I were to keep on saying things like, "Great job! Now you are going to try even harder, aren't you?" or "What a great worker you are! You're a genius in the way you've managed to organize these documents!" well, surely the other person would think I was treating him or her like a child.

外国人は子供っぽいんでしょうか。ともかく誉めてやらないとふ
てくされてしまう。もっと大人になって、じっくりと構えて、そし
て第一に、我々のことを信頼してほしいものです。

分析

日本人はフィードバックが苦手だとよく言われます。フィード
バックとは、相手の仕事やその結果に対して自らの意見や評価を
伝えることを意味します。

欧米に比べて長い時間をかけてじっくりと仕事上の人間関係を
構築しようとする日本人にとって、個々の業務に対して一つ一つ
意見を述べて相手に改善を求めようというスタンスは、むしろ性
急すぎるようにも思えるでしょう。したがって、日本人は欧米人
に比べて部下や同僚のなした成果について、特別なことがないか
ぎり、率直なコメントをしない傾向にあるのです。

特に、相手を誉めることを慎みます。良くできたときは黙って
いても良い関係が続くわけで、それをとりたてて表明する必要は
ないと考えるのでしょう。むしろ何かまずいことがあったとき、
その人と親しい関係にあればあるほど、それを注意し意識を喚起
します。相手が親しい関係にないときは、**知人を介して**その意図
を伝えたりすることもよくあります。減点となる部分を指摘しな
がら改善していき、その中でビジネス上の人間関係を構築しよう
というスタンスをとるのです。

これに対して、欧米、特にアメリカでは、相手が自分のことを
どのように評価しているのか具体的な指摘を求めます。言語や風

Are foreigners really so childish? They seem to **get in a sulk** if you don't keep complimenting them. I'd really like them to become more adult, to present a steady, mature attitude, and above all, to trust that we do appreciate them.

Analysis

The Japanese are often accused of being very poor at giving feedback. "Feedback" refers to the practice of explicitly telling the other person about one's opinion and **evaluation** of his or her work, and the results of this work.

For Japanese, who tend to put quite a bit of effort and time compared to Westerners into steadily building up relations in the workplace, if someone were giving his or her opinions about every bit of work an individual did, trying to get him or her to improve further, it might seem overly demanding. This is one reason that Japanese people tend to comment much less candidly on the achievements of their subordinates or coworkers than their Western counterparts except in special cases.

This is particularly so where praise is concerned. When something is done well, good relations will continue, and it's thought that there's no necessity to actually make special mention of the fact. It's when something is displeasing or not done well that a Japanese will bring it to one's attention and make one conscious of it—and this is all the more true when the relationship is close. Where the relationship with the other person is not particularly close, it's often the case that a Japanese will get what's on his or her mind over to the other person **through an acquaintance**. The idea is to work for improvement by pointing out demerits, and within the context of this to continue to develop a relationship on a business level.

In contrast, in the West, and particularly in America, it's common to ask in no uncertain terms what the other person thinks of one. From the point of view of Americans, who are brought up in a society

俗習慣の違う人々が集まる移民社会に育った彼らから見れば、そうでなければ相手が何を考えているか理解できないのです。

したがって、減点部分のみならず、よかったことを特に指摘し、お互いに向上しようというスタンスで、ビジネス上のコミュニケーションを培っていくのです。

もちろん相手や部下が間違いをおかしたときも、この方法に従って、まず良かったところを指摘した上で、具体的に相手の意見も聞きながら、改善点について話し合います。これは日本のやり方とはかなり異なるものだと言えましょう。

ソリューション

❶ 相手の良いところ、ありがたかったことは積極的に伝えよう。恥ずかしいぐらいに表明するのが適切だ。

❷ 相手の問題点を指摘するときも、まず良いところをほめてから、問題解決の話し合いを建設的に進めよう。あいまいにして日本人だけでこっそりと解決することは慎もう。

❸ フィードバックのテクニックを習得することは、国際間でのビジネスを進めていく上で最も必要な条件だ。外国からのパートナーも交えてしっかりとロールプレイなどで研修しよう。

where people of all sorts of different languages and customs have gathered together, if they didn't do this, they would have no idea what the other person was thinking.

Accordingly, the way they go about things is to help each other to improve by pointing out both demerits and merits—this is the way they **cultivate** good business communication.

Of course, even if a client or subordinate makes a mistake, according to this practice, you should first point out the good parts, listen to the specifics of the person's opinion, and then talk about things that could be improved. This is very different from the Japanese way of doing things.

Solution

❶ Actively talk about the person's good points and your gratitude. It is appropriate to emphasize things to an embarrassing degree.

❷ When pointing out problems, proceed by first praising the good things, and then talk constructively about how to resolve the problem. Refrain from being vague and secretly working on the problems with other Japanese.

❸ Mastering feedback techniques is the most important requirement for doing business internationally. Train to give feedback by thoroughly role-playing with your foreign partners.

5

日本人はなぜもっと自分をアピールして
くれないの？

日本人を見ていると、こいつは仕事ができるのかできないのかわからなくなってしまう。だって、どれだけ能力があって、実務をこなせるのか話してくれないんだから。

外国人の不満　私は、日本に進出しているアメリカ企業の東京支配人です。こちらに来て、気付いたんですが、日本人は、同僚の外国人が仕事ができることをアピールして、それによって昇進したりしようとするととても嫌な顔をするんですよ。ガッツがないというか、自分のキャリアについて、何を考えているかさっぱりわかりません。

　何で自分のことをアピールしてはいけないんだろう？　実力をちゃんと評価してもらうために、これだけのことをやったと堂々と表明することは、ごく当然のことじゃないですか。日本人のようにじっと黙っているんじゃ、その人にどれだけ力があるかなんてわかりゃしない。

　実際、いつも困るのが、日本人を採用しようとして面接をするときだ。彼らは決して自己PRをしない。むしろ何もわかりませんから教えてくださいと言ってくるんで、こっちがびっくりしてしまう。そんな人と会うこと自体、僕にとっちゃ時間の無駄だね。

　そう思うんだけど、逆に今度は僕が日本人に対してどのように自分のことを説明し、実力を認知してもらえばいいのか戸惑っている。いい方法はないものかな。

Why don't Japanese people bring up their strengths more?

> Sometimes it's hard to tell whether a Japanese is really suitable for a job or not. I mean, those guys never say anything explicit about their own abilities, or whether they will be able to handle a job well.

Foreigner's grievance: I'm a manager at the Tokyo branch of an American company that is trying to break into the Japanese market. Since I moved here, I noticed that the Japanese seem to really dislike it when foreign coworkers try to do well for themselves by doing a little bit of self-promotion. Is it because they don't have the guts? I don't understand what they're thinking about their own careers.

Why is it such a bad thing to clearly state one's own abilities? Surely it's natural to **make no bones about** how hard one has worked in order to get someone to make an accurate assessment of one's ability to do a job. When someone just remains silent and doesn't say anything, like the Japanese, how can you get any idea of what that person is capable of?

One of the most trying experiences I have to go through is when I'm giving interviews to Japanese people in order to employ them. They never do any self-promotion. If anything, they stress how little they know and ask me to teach them—which takes me aback somewhat, I can tell you. My view is it's just a waste of time having to see such people.

But then, conversely, I'm at a loss when it comes to telling a Japanese about myself and getting him to recognize my ability. What's the best way of going about things?

日本人の反論　だいたいあなたがたは自己PRが過ぎるんだ。本当に実力のある人は黙っているもんだよ。黙ってたって、その人に実力があれば、自ずとそれは周囲に伝わるもの。そんなに僕はこれができます、私はこんなことを致しましたって言ったって誰が本気にするものかね。みっともないよそれは。だいいち、実際仕事をやらせてみると、口ほどにもないってことも多いじゃないか。

　これは単に個人のPRだけじゃない。製品やサービスの売り込みだってみんなそうだ。だから、外国人のいうことは**話半分に聞いておけ**って我々は思っているんだよ。

分析

　自己を主張して勝ち抜くことをよしとする欧米の人々から見れば、日本人の控えめで謙虚な態度に、時にはいらだたしささえ覚えるはずです。日本には「**能ある鷹は爪を隠す**」という諺があります。日本では自己の能力を披露する人は**安っぽく見られてしまう**というリスクがあるのです。

　自分の能力をできるだけ大きく相手に見せて、それを買ってもらうことによって生き抜いていこうという伝統があるアメリカでは、「能ある鷹」はしっかりと爪を見せなければ、せっかくのチャンスを逸してしまうこともあります。効果的な自己PRも能力の1つだと思われているのです。

　日本では、あまり自分のことを強く主張せずに、仮に相手から誉められても、「そんなことはありませんよ。もっと勉強しなければと思っています」と謙遜して答えれば、あなたの評価はさらにあがっていくはずです。欧米とはまったく違ったアプローチが必要

Japanese retort: Generally speaking, you guys tend to do far too much self-promotion. People with real ability don't brag about it; rather they remain quiet, and if they really do have ability, that fact will naturally communicate itself to the people around. When someone keeps saying, I can do this much, or I did this great thing in the past, who is going to take him seriously? Bluster like that is such bad taste. In the first place, often when you get someone who makes such statements to do a job, you find that in fact they can't do it as well as they say.

And this doesn't only apply to the PR individuals give about themselves—it also applies to sales of goods and services. We Japanese tend to **take** foreigners' bragging **with a pinch of salt**.

Analysis

For Western people, who value coming through and winning through self-assertion, the attitude of retiring modesty in many Japanese is sometimes almost irritating. In Japan, there is a saying that "**the clever hawk hides its talons**." In Japan, any person who keeps on drawing attention to his or her own ability runs the risk of being thought of as **undignified**.

In the States, it's traditionally thought that the way to survive is by showing one's ability to others in as bold a way as possible to get them to believe in you. If you hide your talons, you will probably end up missing out on precious opportunities! Effective self-promotion is considered a vital element of a person's abilities.

In Japan, one makes a much better impression on others if one does not assert oneself too much, and makes sure to reply modestly even if one is praised by someone else—saying "No, no, there's so much more I have to learn." It's completely the opposite approach from the one that is used in the United States.

になるわけです。

　だから、日本人は、海外の人と働くとき、しっかりと自分が何をしてきたかを説明できるよう、まず文章にまとめておくことも必要です。できるだけ具体的に、このプロジェクトをオーガナイズしたとか、こうした製品開発にかかわったとか、言葉では言いにくい部分を情報としてまとめて、しっかりと自分の方から伝達するようにつとめましょう。

　また、外国人は、日本人が自らを謙遜することを伝統的な美徳と思っていることを理解して、その人の実力を前もって他の人から聞いておくなどの情報収集をしておくことをお薦めします。自分のPRを英語でどんどん語る人より、一見おとなしい人の方が、日本でのビジネスには向いていることもあるんですよ。

ソリューション

❶ 日本人のビジネス文化に謙遜を美徳とする風習があることを、具体的な事例で海外のパートナーに伝えておこう。

❷ 自らのアピールをしっかりと行うことは、欧米とビジネスをする上でのニーズであることを理解しよう。

❸ ほめられたときは謙遜せずに、「Thank you!!」の一言で相手の賛辞に応えよう。

For that reason, it's necessary to **put things in writing** so that you can explain clearly what you did when Japanese people work with foreigners. Write as specifically as possible about how you organized this project, or were involved in the development of that product, writing down the things that are difficult to say, and making an effort to convey clearly what you want to communicate.

Also, it is recommended that foreigners be aware that modesty has traditionally been considered a personal virtue among the Japanese, so they should try to collect information in advance about the Japanese person's ability, etc. by listening to other people. People who seem to be quiet might be more suitable for business in Japan those than those who are always promoting themselves in English.

Solution

❶ Explain to your foreign partners, using specific examples, that modesty is considered a virtue in Japan's business culture.

❷ Understand that talking about one's own strengths is a necessity in Western business culture.

❸ When someone praises you, do not be modest. Respond to the person's compliment with a "Thank you!"

日本人のほほえみって不気味だよ。本心が わからないんだよ。

> 日本人の表情からは何を思っているのか推測できない。笑っているのか と思っていると実は怒っていたり……。彼らはなぜあんなに自分を隠そ うとするんだろう?

外国人の不満 　私は、ニューヨークの本社でマーケティングを担当し ています。日本に出張して、会議なんかでこちらがプレゼンテーシ ョンをするときに、よく日本人は顔に笑みを浮かべているんです。 あの表情に接するととても**不愉快な**気分になります。

例えば私がこの提案についてどう思いますかって聞くと、往々に してそうした笑みにぶつかってしまう。最初は何がおかしいんだろ うって思ったんですが、何度も経験しているうちに、あれは日本人 特有の**皮肉**なんだってことに気付きました。本当は提案に反対なの に、にんまりと笑って無視してしまう。

反対なら反対ってはっきりと言えばいいのに、そうはしない。そ んな日本人の対応を見ていると、こちらが侮辱されているような気 がしてしまうんです。何とか日本人の本当の意見や思いを聞き出す ことはできないんでしょうか?

日本人の反論 　我々から見ると、欧米の人間こそ**含蓄**がなくぶっきら ぼうで失礼だ。うまくオブラートにくるんで相手に物事を伝えるこ とをせずに、常にじっと我々の目を見て迫ってくる。しかも大げさ なジェスチャーでね。

そんなにまでしなくても、以心伝心というのがあってね、相手を

The faint smiles on Japanese people's faces are creepy. I really don't understand them.

> You can never tell from a Japanese person's face what he or she is thinking. You think they're smiling but in fact they're quite mad at you. Why do they have to hide themselves like that?

Foreigner's grievance: I do marketing at our headquarters in New York. When I go on business trips to Japan, in conferences and suchlike, when one of us is making a presentation, often we'll see faint smiles on the Japanese faces. I find it **repellant** to have to see that kind of expression.

For example, I may be asking someone what he thinks of a proposal I've made, and often I'll be met with the same kind of smile. My first reaction was to think "What's so funny?" But after experiencing this kind of smile quite a few times, I realized that this reaction must represent a peculiarly Japanese kind of **sarcasm**. Really the guy's opposed to the proposal, but he'll just ignore it and give a complacent smile.

If he doesn't agree with it, why doesn't he just say so? But he doesn't. It's humiliating to be treated like this. Is there a way one can get Japanese people to tell you their thoughts and opinions straight out?

Japanese retort: To us, Westerners sometimes seem far too direct, plain rude, in fact—and quite unable to appreciate **implications**. They don't take the trouble to communicate things to the other person with the appropriate kind of delicacy, but come bearing down on us, staring us straight in the eyes—and with such exaggerated gestures.

You don't have to thrust it down our throat, you know. And

傷つけることなく、やんわりと拒絶したり、反対したりすることこそ、マナーを心得た社会人と言えるんじゃないですか。それをいちいち、目をむいて、相手にどうだと迫られたんじゃどうにもなりませんね。

そんなときは、我々は大人げなく不満を表明するのもどうかと思って微笑みで応えるんですよ。これって日本人ならわかるでしょ、苦笑いなんですよ。

分析

　欧米、特にアメリカ人と日本人とのコミュニケーション・スタイルの際だった違いの1つに**表情の問題**があります。

　ビジネスの場などで、人と誠意をもって交流しなければならないとき、アメリカ人は自らの思いと表情とを一致させることを常識と考えます。真剣なことを話すときは真剣な表情を、喜びを表現するときや、不快を表明するときも、ちゃんとそれに対応した明るい表情や不愉快な表情をもって接するわけです。これがアメリカ人にとっての誠意なのです。よくポーカーフェイスという言葉があるように、難しい状況でも平気な顔をするというケースもありますが、これはあくまでも自らの精神力の強さを示すもので、相手と通常のコミュニケーションを行う場合にする表情ではありません。

　さて、それに対して日本人はどうでしょう。日本人は心の中と表情とを一致させることは、ともすれば大人げないと考えます。日本流の礼儀を心得た大人なら、誰でもそんなに大らかに自分の

sometimes words are unnecessary, anyway. Refusing or opposing something in a mild way, a way that doesn't hurt the other person's feelings—isn't this a requirement in the behavior of an adult who understands what good manners entail? When somebody comes at you asking what you think, looking you straight in the eye and pointing at you with a forefinger in your face, it's hard to know how to deal with him.

On such occasions, we don't want to tell them how distasteful we find it—that would be too immature—so we just reply with a faint smile. This is what we call a "pained" or "bitter" smile—any Japanese would understand it.

Analysis

One very significant difference between the communication styles of Japanese and Westerners, particularly Americans, lies in **facial expressions**.

In the work place and other situations, and especially when people are interacting with one another with sincerity, Americans regard it as common sense to make one's facial expression match one's thoughts. When you're talking about something serious, you should have a serious expression; when you express joy or displeasure, you should make your facial expression match accordingly, putting on a cheerful face or a displeased face as appropriate. This is sincerity, according to Americans. There is a word, "poker-face," which refers to the expression a person might put on when he or she maintains a bland expression even when placed in a difficult situation. But this is taken to denote psychological strength, and it doesn't represent the kind of expression one should have ordinarily when communicating with another person.

Now, what about the Japanese view? Japanese people tend to think that letting one's face become a direct reflection of one's emotions, plainly showing what is on one's mind, is not appropriately adult

気持ちを表情には出しません。長い歴史を通して、自らの感情を
ぐっと心に留めておくことを美徳としてきた日本人は、ずっと微
妙な表情や笑みで、相手に自らの意図をやんわりと伝えてきまし
た。

　そうです、欧米の人と日本人とでは相手に対する誠意ある気持
ちの表現方法そのものが異なるのです。このことは外国人も日本
人も十分に理解しておきたいものです。心と表情を一致させる国
から来た人は、往々にして表情だけでなくボディ・ランゲージも
大きくなり、相手に対するアイコンタクトも強くなりがちです。
そして日本人はそのまったく逆の対応をしてしまいます。ビジネ
ス上の真剣勝負であればあるほど、そうした対応の仕方が際立っ
てくることに大きな誤解の原因があるのです。

ソリューション

❶ 思いと表情を一致させるように心がけよう。苦笑い、皮肉っぽい曖昧な笑
みは誤解のもと。うれしさ、悲しさ、そして怒りも率直に表そう。

❷ 海外のパートナーの誤解を事前に防ぐためにも、日本人の表情が曖昧で、
ジェスチャーも大きくないことを、事前にオリエンテーションしておこ
う。それも楽しくフレンドリーに。

❸ 英語を話すときは、英語にあったボディ・ランゲージを習得し、できるだ
け実践しよう。恥ずかしがらずに鏡でも見て、役者のつもりで練習してみ
よう。

behavior. No one who is an adult, and who understands what is considered good manners in Japan, allows his or her own feelings to appear too easily on his or her face. For many centuries in Japan, keeping one's feelings absolutely under control, hidden deep within one's breast, was considered a **virtue**. So Japanese have long been used to communicating their intentions to the other person in a roundabout way, with subtle facial expressions and smiles.

That's right, it's precisely here, in the method of expressing one's sincerity to another person, that a great difference lies between Westerners and Japanese. This is something that both foreigners and Japanese would do well to take note of. People who come from countries where it's common to make one's face match one's emotions tend to use bolder gestures too, and to look others straight in the eye. Japanese, however, will respond by doing precisely the opposite. And often, in business, the more serious a contest or battle is, the more apparent these differences become something that often leads to great misunderstanding.

Solution

❶ Keep in mind that your expressions should match your thoughts and emotions. Bitter smiles and ironic, vague smiles can cause misunderstandings. Show happiness, sadness, and even anger clearly.

❷ In order to prevent your foreign partner from misunderstanding things, have an orientation session beforehand about vague Japanese facial expressions and not making large gestures. It should be friendly and fun.

❸ Practice as often as possible to acquire body language that is suitable to your words when speaking English. Look at yourself in the mirror without being shy and practice as if you were an actor.

Business is business、
あなたたちわかってるの?

日本人に反対意見を伝えたりすると、その場だけでなくあとあとまで人間関係にしこりが残ったりする。ビジネス上の意見交換なのに、どうして彼らは、そんなに根に持つんだろうか?

外国人の不満　私は、東京の外資系企業に**現地採用**されたカナダ人です。日本に留学して、こちらで就職したので、日本のことはわかっているつもりだったのですが、最近日本人とどのようにつき合ったらいいかわからなくなることがあるんです。とういうのも、本気でビジネス上の討議をしようとすればするほど相手との溝が深くなるような気がしてならないんです。

　だってね、ビジネスの場においては率直に意見を言うことが何よりも大切なことでしょ。それなのに、意見を言えば言うほど、日本人は殻の中に閉じこもってしまい私を避けようとするんです。時には何もかもあいまいにして、その後**なしのつぶて**になってしまったり。最悪の時は、いきなり感情的になって中傷したりするんです。ビジネスはビジネスじゃないですか。ビジネスの場でちゃんと自分の意見を表明しなくて、いったいどのようにして建設的な意見交換ができるというんでしょうか。

　彼らは心の奥底では外国人を受け入れようとしていない気がしてなりません。それならそれでいい。こちらは自分のニーズは伝えて、相手がそれに対応しなかったんだから、それは日本側の責任ということになっちゃうでしょ。もっと真摯に我々の意見や思いを受けとめてもらいたいものです。

Business is business.
Do you understand that?

Often when you let a Japanese know that you disagree with him or her, some difficult feeling remains between you for a long time afterwards. It's only an exchange of opinions in business matters, so why take it personally?

Foreigner's grievance: I'm a Canadian **local hire** at a for-eign-owned company in Tokyo. I went to school and was hired in Japan, so I thought I understood Japan, but recently, there have been times I just didn't know how to deal with the Japanese. The more earnest I get in a business discussion with a Japanese, the more a rift seems to form between us.

I mean, surely it's vital to be able to be frank in one's exchange of opinions in the workplace, isn't it? But the more I say what I think, the more the Japanese will retreat back inside their shell and try to avoid me. Occasionally, the conversation will just get very vague, and the discussion will **peter out into nothing**, with no result. At worst, the Japanese will suddenly get very emotional and start to insult me. But business is business, isn't it? If people can't express their opinions in business situations, how can we expect to have a constructive exchange?

I can't help feeling that in their heart of hearts, the Japanese just don't want to accept us. If that's the case, well so be it. If we're trying to get our needs across, and they're not going to listen, then that's their responsibility. I wish they would listen to our opinions and thoughts less emotionally, though.

日本人の反論 欧米の人は我々がどう対応してよいかわからないくらい、すぐに明解な答えを求めてくる。これにはうんざりです。そしてうまくコミュニケーションがいかなくなれば、すぐに突っかかってくる。しかもですよ、そんな深刻なミーティングをした後、あたかも何もなかったかのように、ニコニコして冗談を言ったりするんです。これには我々はなかなかついていけませんよ。

だってですよ、目をむいて、例の大きなジェスチャーでこっちの意見をさんざんこき下ろしておいて、その後しゃあしゃあと冗談を交わすなんて、あまりにも人を馬鹿にしていませんか。

我々は常に相手を傷つけまいとして、慎重に、優しく対応しているんですよ。それなのに彼らときたら、そうした我々の苦労を全く意に介さない。いったいどうなっているんでしょう。

分析

事例3でも説明しましたね。ビジネス上の意見交換を行うとき、日本人と欧米の人との間には、コミュニケーションのあり方に根本的なスタンスの違いがあるんです。

欧米の人はビジネス上の意見を相手に伝えることは、あたかも手に持ったボールを相手に投げるようなものだと考えます。すなわち、意見を**キャッチボール**のように交換して、よりよいアイデアを模索しようとするのです。ビジネス上の議論は、あくまでもキャッチボールであって、相手の心に対してボールを投げつけているのではないのです。だからこそ、強い反対意見でも、日本人から見ると比較的簡単な気持ちで表明できるのです。そして、それはあくまでもビジネス上のキャッチボールなのですから、それが終われば、あとはさらっとして冗談を交わしたり、楽しい食事

Japanese retort: Westerners always want a clear answer on the spot, right then and there. This is the first thing that really gets to us. And then when we can't give them the on-the-spot answer that they want, they come and attack us immediately. And also, when the meeting that was so full of tension is over, now they come up to us all smiling and jokey, just as if nothing had happened, and want to have a chat. Well, sorry, but we just can't do that. What do you mean, why?

You know. A guy who has been contemptuously **putting down** my every suggestion, rolling his eyes and making exaggerated gestures at me, now comes up amiably and wants to exchange pleasantries? What kind of a person does he take me for?

We do our best to be cautious and polite in the way we deal with them, always trying not to hurt the other guy's feelings, but our efforts don't mean a thing to them. What is going on here?

Analysis

We talked about this in Case 3. It would be as well for you both to be aware of a fundamental difference in positions in communication methods between Japanese and Westerners when it comes to exchanges of opinions in matters of business.

Westerners regard telling someone else one's opinion on business matters as comparable throwing a ball across to another person. In other words, Americans exchange opinions as if they were **playing catch** with one another—this is how they try to help each other develop better ideas. Debates on business matters are like playing catch: opinions aren't thrown at the other person with the idea of aiming for his or her heart or emotions. Even opinions that are strongly in disagreement can be voiced relatively easily, from the Japanese point of view. And since it is only a game of ball in business matters, when it's over jokes can be exchanged and people can have meals together, just as if nothing has happened.

をしたりといったことができるのです。

では日本人はどうでしょう。日本人はビジネス上の意見交換とはいえ、それを決してキャッチボールとは捉えません。人間関係や上下関係、さらにはそれぞれの立場を気遣いながら、慎重に意見を交換することを**よしとする**日本人は、相手の意見に強く反対した場合、得てして相手を中傷していると捉えがちなのです。

特に日本人は相手とより良い人間関係を構築しながらビジネス上の打ち合わせを進めようとします。したがって、まだ人間関係が十分でない相手からいきなり反対意見を表明された場合、戸惑ってしまい、対応ができなくなってしまうのです。

さらに言うならば、ビジネス上の会話を自分の感情と切り放して進めることに、日本人は**精神的に大変な抵抗**があるのです。すなわち、相手が自分に反対してくると、日本人はそれをハートで受けとめてしまいがちです。相手のボールをグローブをはめた手で受け取って、相手に投げ返すかわりに、心にそれがどんとぶつかって、相手に対する不信感や怒りに転化されてしまうことがあるのです。日本人はそうしたリスクを避けるため、やんわりと相手に対応したり、時にはもっとリラックスして話のできるお酒の席などで本音を相手に伝えます。

しかし、そうした日本人の心理は欧米の人にはなかなか理解してもらえません。欧米の人が日本でビジネス上の意見交換をする上で是非知っておかなければならないことは、こうした日本人の精神風土を理解して、自らの意見を表明する前に、できるだけ相手側と非公式な意見交換の場をもっておくことです。それも会議

Now, what about the Japanese? Japanese people will never be able to treat an exchange of opinions, even if it is one about business matters, as simply as a game of catch. Japanese people **set great store by** a careful exchange of opinions, undertaken in a way that is mindful of the particular relationships that exist between the people involved, the differences in rank, and also the particular position of each party involved. So disagreeing or opposing another person's opinion too vehemently tends, in most cases, to be taken as insulting to the other person.

In particular, the Japanese usually like to hold meetings about business matters while building up better relationships with the other person. So if someone with whom they have not yet built up a thorough relationship expresses an opinion that is in direct opposition to theirs, they get confused and become unable to deal with the situation.

Furthermore, Japanese people have **great psychological resistance** to holding business discussions in a way that is cut off from their own emotions. That is to say, a Japanese will often tend to take it to heart when a person to whom he or she is talking contradicts him or her outright. Instead of just catching the other person's opinion in a gloved hand and throwing another one back, the opinion hits the Japanese person deeply in the heart. Then it gets turned into distrust and anger at the other person. In order to avoid this kind of situation, Japanese tend to deal with the other person by expressing opinions in an indirect way, occasionally letting the other person know their true opinion in a place that is set apart from the workplace, where both parties can relax over a meal or a drink.

But this kind of psychology is quite hard for Westerners to understand. Westerners should know that to have an effective exchange of opinions in Japan it is vital to be aware of the particular emotional make-up of the Japanese in this area, and thus to arrange unofficial occasions where opinions can be exchanged frankly with the other side before finalizing their own opinions. That, too, rather than being a meeting, should take place in an informal setting. In that way, they

などではなく、リラックスして話せる場で。そして、お互いにフランクに意見交換ができるような人間関係の構築にまず努力し、そこから徐々にビジネス上の交流を進めていくよう、心がけるとよいでしょう。

ソリューション

❶ 海外からのパートナーに、公式な会議の前後の場を変えた打ち合わせがいかに重要か説明しておこう。ちょうど、国連や議員へのロビー活動を引き合いにだしてわかりやすく。「根回し」という言葉を英語でうまく説明するのも一案かも。

❷ ビジネスの場での会話はあくまでもビジネス上のこと。個人攻撃ではないことをしっかりと理解して打ち合わせに臨むべし。もちろん感情で相手に挑むのは愚の骨頂だ。

❸ その場で何もかも一挙に解決しようとせず、キャッチボールをするようなコミュニケーションの中からソリューションを導くことが、海外とのビジネスでは重要なテクニック。面倒に思わずに、場数を踏んで研修しよう。

will be able to work to build up the kind of relationship where each side feels able to exchange opinions frankly, and only after that slowly and steadily try to work towards creating exchanges on business matters.

Solution

❶ Explain to your partners from abroad about the importance of informal get-togethers before and after the formal meetings. It will be easy for them to understand if you bring up lobbyists' activities at the United Nations and for Parliamentarians and Congresspersons. One way is to explain the word "nemawashi" clearly in English.

❷ Conversations in a place of business are about business. When having discussions, you should understand clearly that they are not personal attacks. Of course, there is nothing more foolish than to speak emotionally to the person you are talking to.

❸ An important technique used by foreign business people is to arrive at a solution through a communication style that is like "playing catch" without trying to solve everything at once on the spot. Practice it over and over and avoid thinking of it as a nuisance.

事例

8

おいおい、日本人さん、 そんなに緊張しないでよ。

日本人に会ってビジネスの話をするとき、こっちが相手と気軽に意見交換しようとしてカジュアルになればなるほど、日本人は固く、そして頑なになってしまう。なにかとても緊張しているようなので、こっちまでやばいのかなって思ってしまうよ。

外国人の不満 私の故郷テキサスでは、ボスはとてもおだやかで、いつもにこにこ。そして机に足をおいて、のんびりと話してくれる。ところが、日本ではそうはいかないんだ。

日本人とビジネスの話をするときに困るのが、日本人が無表情で、すぐに堅苦しい表情や姿勢で接してくることです。ジェスチャーが少ないとか、英語がうまく話せないとか、そういうことなら理解できる。でも、そうではなくて、いかにも不快そうにじっとして、しかもどんどん無口になっていく。そして時々日本人だけでこそこそと話をして、一言二言ことばを返してくるだけ。これでは話し合いなんてできやしない。

いったい、日本人はどうしてあんなに**緊張している**んでしょうか。いくら文化が違うからって、日本人同士ならばもう少しうまくやっているんでしょう? 我々は別にあなた方に**攻撃をしかけている**わけじゃない。ただ、できるだけオープンに、そしてカジュアルに話し合いたいと思っているだけなんです。

日本人の反論 欧米の人たちのあの横柄な態度はなんなのでしょう。最初からこちらを威圧するつもりなんでしょうかね。椅子に座って足を組むぐらいならいいのですが、**だらんと座って片手を椅子の背**

Hey there, Japanese people, don't be so nervous.

> When we meet with Japanese and talk business, the more casual we are in our attempts to make the others relax and discuss things freely, the more obstinately formal the Japanese seem to get.

Foreigner's grievance: Where I come from in Texas, the boss was really genial, and always had a smile on his face. He'd put his feet up on his desk and would talk to you **in an easy manner**.

But in Japan, it's not that way at all. I find it so difficult when I'm talking business with the Japanese: their faces remain expressionless and they act so stiff and formal. I could tolerate it if it were just a matter of their not gesturing very much, or not being able to speak English very well. But no, they just look so uptight and uncomfortable, and sit there so stiffly, getting more and more silent. Sometimes they might whisper among themselves and come back with one or two sentences, but there's no hope in hell of having a good discussion like that.

Why do they have to be so **uptight**? Okay, so they're having to deal with a different culture, but surely the Japanese manage to have better discussions when they are by themselves? We're not trying to **launch an attack** against you guys particularly. We just want to have as open-hearted and casual a discussion as we possibly can.

Japanese retort: What makes Westerners think that they can behave so arrogantly? They want to make us feel small from the start—is that it? Okay, so we can take it when they sit down and cross their legs, but when they sit in such a **sloppy way** with their legs out

にかけたりして、あれではあたかもやくざの親分とでも話している
かのようです。しかも英語でどんどん主張してくるから、こちらと
してはとても対応できやしません。ましてうちの若手なんか、そん
な相手の態度にびくびくするし、気の強い者は腹をたてて憮然とす
るし……。

あれはコミュニケーション以前の問題ですね。きっと、自分たち
が正しくて、自分たちのことを聞いていればいいんだと彼らは思っ
ているんでしょう。

分析

ビジネスでのコミュニケーション上の誤解は、実は些細なことか
らはじまり、傷口を広げていくものです。典型的な例が、相手に対
してどのような印象を持つかという、いわゆる相手に対する評価が
原因で、お互いの交流がうまくいかなくなるケースでしょう。

よく欧米の人は相手と仕事の話をするときでも、できるだけカ
ジュアルな雰囲気で、リラックスして話をしようとします。ある
意味で、それは彼らにとっての礼儀のようなもので、背筋を正し
て堅苦しい話をするのではなく、**打ち解けた雰囲気**をつくって、
アイデアを交換したいという思いからそうした対応をとるのです。
ゆったりと椅子に腰掛けて、足を組んだり、時には机の上に足を
のせたり。

ところが、どちらかというとフォーマリティを重んじる日本人
からみれば、こうしたスタイルは実に横柄で高圧的にすら思えま
す。人の話は謙虚に聞くべきだという価値観を子供の時から植え
付けられてきた日本人にしてみると、ゆったりと座って、手を椅
子の背にまわすといったようなジェスチャーからは、カジュアル
どころか威圧のメッセージしか受け取りません。したがって、そ

and rest an arm along the back of their chair, it feels just like we're having a discussion with some gangland boss. Then they talk and talk at us in English—how do they expect us to be able to handle it? The younger ones among us get nervous in the face of people with that kind of attitude, while the bolder ones simply get angry and astonished.

The problem is not simply a matter of communication. I'm sure they think they're in the right, that if we just listen to what they tell us everything will be solved.

Analysis

Misunderstandings in business communication in fact usually arise in the smallest matters, and then the wounds just keep getting bigger. Typical examples are cases where exchanges between two parties break down because of differences in the evaluation they make of each other, and the kind of impression they want to make.

Often when Westerners are talking with each other about work, they try as much as possible to do it casually, and talk in a relaxed way. In a sense, this is good form for them: they adopt this way of coping with the situation out of the desire for an exchange of ideas in an open, **relaxed atmosphere** rather than in a stiff, formal discussion. So they sit in a relaxed fashion in their chairs, cross their legs, and sometimes even put their legs on the desk, etc.

However, to the Japanese, who tend to put a high priority on formality, this kind of style appears arrogant, and even threatening. From childhood most Japanese have the idea planted in them that they should listen to people's comments with a respectful attitude, so if someone puts his arm on the back of his chair, rather than seeming like a relaxed gesture it seems like a threatening one. Accordingly, in such a situation the Japanese will become more and more stiff and

うした場にでると日本人はますます固くなり、緊張したり、時には腹を立てたりということになってしまうのです。

　もちろん、逆もまた真なりで、日本人のそうした固い姿勢を欧米の人は、拒絶のサインと捉えてしまうリスクもあるのです。たかが姿勢、されど姿勢というわけで、こうしたことから生まれる誤解は相手の人格への評価に繋がるだけに、より根深いものになってしまうのです。双方ともが相手の習慣をよく理解して、お互いの真意を誤解されないように努めるべきでしょう。

ソリューション

❶ 欧米の人の大きなジェスチャーや強い視線を脅威と思うな。これは単なる習慣の違い。日本人も相手の目を見て、堂々とした態度で応対するよう練習しよう。

❷ 上下関係があっても、ある程度カジュアルに、フレンドリーに対応するよう心がけよう。上司が部下の机に座って話をしたり、机に足をのせて話をするのはリラックスした雰囲気をつくろうとしてのこと。おどおどするなかれ。

❸ 声の小さい人は、少し大きな声で。英語がわからないときは、わからないことをちゃんと表明しても大丈夫。ゆっくり話してくれとニーズを伝え、自分のペースを維持して対応しよう。

tense, and sometimes get very angry.

But the converse applies too: this stiffness from the Japanese holds the risk of seeming like a sign of refusal to Americans. Okay, it's only one's posture, you might say, but it's important—and in as much as the misunderstandings that arise from such things can be linked to the way people evaluate someone's character, they are in fact of much deeper significance. Both sides should try and be more understanding about each other's customs, and work hard so that no misunderstandings arise about each other's real intentions.

Solution

❶ Do not think that the big gestures and direct gazes of foreigners are threats. It is just a different custom. Japanese people should also practice looking others in the eye and having a dignified attitude.

❷ Keep in mind that even when there is a superior-subordinate relationship, you should be casual and friendly to some degree. When the boss sits and talks at a subordinate's desk or puts his or her feet up on a desk, it creates a relaxed atmosphere. Do not let it intimidate you.

❸ If you are a quiet talker, try to speak in a louder voice. When you do not understand something in English, it is okay to express that you could not catch the person's meaning. Tell people that you need them to speak slowly and proceed at your own pace.

言っていることが
わからないよ、
日本人

ROUND **2**

I Don't Understand What You're
Saying, Japanese People

事例

9

そんなことを聞いているんじゃないよ。 ## ちゃんと質問に答えてくれ！

> いったい、日本人は我々の言っていることがわかっているのでしょうか？
> だって、尋ねた問いとはまったく違った、無関係な答えが返ってきて煙
> にまかれることがしょっちゅうあるんだ。

外国人の不満　僕はロサンゼルスで財務の仕事をしています。関係会
社が日本にあるのですが、東京に出張して、何か重要な課題を日本
側と進めようとすると、いつも不可思議なことが起きるんですよ。

　例えば、「今年度の予算だけどね。この経費の部分、3分の1に削
ることはできないだろうか」って尋ねたとするでしょ。すると、僕が
予測しているのとまったく異なった、**思いも寄らない答え**が返って
くる。「3年前にこのプロジェクトを始めたときは、ほんのわずかな
人数で頑張ったものだよ」なんていう答えがね。だって、コストを節
約することと、3年前にプロジェクトを始めたときのことといったい
どこにつながりがあるんだろう。

　だから僕は、「ちょっと待って、コストは削減できるのどうなの」
って問いつめる。すると、また同じような答えが返ってくる。僕は
混乱して、はっきりとした答えを改めて要求すると、いきなりぶっ
きらぼうに「わかったよ、そうしますよ」って言われたりする。彼が
本当に納得したとは思えないのに、結局彼の本当の気持ちを聞き出
すことなく、会話が終わってしまうんだよ。なにか、後味の悪さば
かりが残るんだ。

　なんで日本人はストレートに対応してくれないんだろう。何かは
っきりと言えないような事情があるんだろうか？

日本人の反論　彼らはともかく、自分の意見を押しつけることしか考
えていない。だって、こちらが何か理由を説明しようとすると、最

That isn't what I asked you. Answer my question first!

Do Japanese people really understand what we ask them? So often an answer comes back from them that is completely at cross-purposes to the question that we've posed, so we find ourselves unable to progress any further.

Foreigner's grievance: I work at a financial firm in Los Angeles. One of our affiliated companies is in Japan, so I make business trips to Tokyo. Whenever I bring up an important topic to the Japanese people, something strange happens.

For example, if I say, "Okay, let's talk about this year's budget. Do you think we can pare down the estimated costs here by about a third?" I then get a totally **off-the-wall** answer, quite unrelated to anything I expected. A reply like, "Well, three years ago, when we started this project, we tried our very best, and there were only a handful of us." I mean, what relevance does whatever happened at the start of the project have to our trying to economize on costs?

Then I say, "Hey, wait a minute, what about what I said, paring down expenditure?" But all I get is the very same answer! Then I get confused, and again demand an answer to what I asked—and suddenly he flares up and says straight out, "Okay, okay. We'll do as you say." It's obvious he doesn't really want to go along with me, but the conversation ends without my being able to hear what he truly thinks about the subject. And then all I'm left with is a bad feeling.

Why don't Japanese people come back at me with a straight answer? Is there a reason for their being unable to reply in a clear manner?

Japanese retort: All those guys ever think about is making us agree with their opinions. I mean, I'll be trying to explain the reason why

後まで聞こうとせずに、途中で割り込んできてかき回して、最後には自分の考えを**押し通してしまう**んだ。これじゃあ会話はできないね。「あんたが大将。好きにしな」って言いたくなるよ。

どうして、彼らは真摯に日本人から情報をとろうとしないんだろう。こっちは親切に問題となっていることがらの背景をひもといて、理解してもらおうって努力しているのに、彼らは我々の事情なんて最初から興味ないんだよ。

分析

このやりとりは、日本人と外国人、特に英語圏の人とがビジネス上のコミュニケーションを公式な場などで口頭でとろうとするとき、必ずといっていいほど発生する深刻な問題です。実に簡単なトリックに両者ともひっかかって、相互に不信の念をつのらせていくのです。

日本人は何か説明しなければならないときに、まず**背景**から説きおこし、物事の核心へむかって解説をしようとします。この事例も、3年前の事情から始めて、現在の状況へと話を進め、最終的に「だから予算のカットはもう少し延期してもらいたい」といったような結論を導きだそうとしていたのです。

これに対して、外国人は**結論をはっきりと先に表明**し、その後で理由を説明し、相手に理解してもらおうとします。背景から説明し、結論に至ろうとする日本人のロジックそのものが、外国人のスピーチの手順には存在しないのです。外国人から見ると、自分の問いとはまったく無関係の話をいきなり持ち出され戸惑ってしまうのです。

we can or can't do such a thing, but they don't bother to hear me out. They interrupt me halfway through, putting their oar in, and then finally they'll simply **plough ahead** with what they're thinking anyway. What kind of way is that to hold a conversation? I often want to blurt out, "Okay, you think you're the boss—you make the decision."

Why are they not more willing to listen to the information we Japanese will be trying to give them around a situation? We'll be trying with goodwill to unravel the background to whatever has become a problem, trying to get it across to them, but right from the start they'll show no interest in what we're saying.

Analysis

In this exchange, we see a serious problem that nearly always arises in verbal business communication in situations such as formal discussions between Japanese and foreigners, especially of the English-speaking world. A simple catch is tripping up both parties in mid-course and increasing mutual distrust and suspicion.

When Japanese have to explain something, they start by evoking the **background circumstances,** and only gradually go on to get to the core of the problem. In this case, the speaker was going to start by explaining various circumstances in the company three years ago, and he would have gone on to talk about the present state of affairs, and from there finally to reach his point, which was "So I'd prefer that you put off cost-cutting for a while."

In contrast, foreigners **put their conclusions first**, in a clear-cut way, and only after that, in an attempt to get the other person to understand, do they explain the reasons. The structural logic of the Japanese, who start by explaining the background and then go on to their conclusion, does not exist in the **modus operandi** of foreign discourse. From the non-Japanese point of view, it's confusing when the person they are speaking to starts talking about something that

　日本人が**起承転結法**に則って話をした場合などは、特にそうした行き違いが起こってしまい、意見交換が思うようにいかなくなってしまいます。

　しかも、欧米の人はそうした困惑を解消するときに、相手の話を途中で遮ってでも明解な答えを求めようとします。これも、欧米の人から見れば当然のマナーなのですが、日本人から見れば人の話を途中で遮って、自分の意見を押しつけるということになってしまうのでしょう。結局、話の核心が見えない外国人が、自分の意見をしっかり表明しようとして、さらなる悪循環を生み出してしまうのです。

　欧米の人にぜひ薦めたいことは、日本人は往々にして結論を最後に表明するので、忍耐強く、話を遮らずに最後まで相手の言うことを聞き出すというアプローチをもつことです。

　そして、日本人も、できるだけ、まず最も言いたい結論を最初に明解に表明するか、あるいは相手が割り込んできても**動じずに**、そこで改めて結論を強調するといったスタンスが必要なのです。

ソリューション

❶ 最も強調したいポイントから話していこう。できれば、ポイントを文章にして、パワーポイントなどで見せながらプレゼンをすれば、英語のハンディキャップも補える。

❷ 外国人は往々にして、話の途中でもわからないことや、好奇心をかきたてられると割り込んでくる。これは彼らの文化。気にせず、ペースを乱されないよう注意しよう。

❸ 最初に、質疑応答は最後にまとめて行いますと言うと、相手は割り込まずに聞いてくれる。それでも割り込まれたら、最後まで聞いてくれとこちらから注意しよう。

seems so completely irrelevant to the question that they've asked.

When Japanese people talk using the traditional rhetorical method of "**Introduction, Development, Turn, and Conclusion**," this sort of misunderstanding arises particularly frequently, making it impossible to have a useful exchange of opinions.

Furthermore, Westerners usually try to deal with their confusion by stopping the other person in mid-speech and demanding clarification. From a Westerner's point of view, this is not bad manners; it's simply a matter of necessity. But to Japanese, it seems like you are interrupting someone else's speech so you can force your own opinion on them. In the end, the foreigner, who fails to see the central point, simply tries even more forcefully to make his own point clearer, and the problem keeps repeating itself and getting worse.

One thing I would really like to suggest to foreigners is that they try to listen patiently to what other people have to say without interrupting, since Japanese people progress slowly and steadily, and only get to their central point last.

To the Japanese, I would say that you should try to give a clear indication at the start of your speech about what you will be trying to say. And try **not to be flummoxed** when the other person interrupts you: simply stress once more, clearly, the main point of what you are trying to say.

Solution

❶ Talk about the point that you want to emphasize first. If possible, write your points down, and make your presentation using something like PowerPoint®. This will help you overcome the handicap of speaking in English.

❷ It is often the case that foreigners will interrupt you in the middle of speaking to ask about something they do not understand or are curious about. This is their culture. Do not worry about it, and be careful not to let it throw you off.

❸ When you begin, if you tell people that you will take questions at the end, they will listen to you without interrupting. If you are still interrupted, ask the person to listen until you have finished.

事例

10

プレゼンテーションの勉強をすべきだよ、日本人は。

日本人はなんであんなにスピーチが下手なのだろう？ 言っていることも論理的ではなく、自信もなさそう。あれじゃあ、ビジネスでしっかりと相手を説得することは不可能だ。

外国人の不満　私は、ロンドンから日本に送られてきた営業関係の責任者です。いつも、日本の部下にちゃんとわかりやすい発表をするよう言うのですが、なかなかうまくいきません。

　まず**論理性がない**んです。日本人は自分の意見を述べるときに、もっと合理的なロジックに従ってアプローチしてもらいたい。自信をもって、言いたいことをはっきりと表明してもらわなければ、その人が本当に**やる気**があるのか、心からそのように思っているのかわからなくなります。

　日本人は話をするときに、いつもどこかおどおどして自信がなさそうに見えます。時には、なにか特別なことを隠しているんじゃないかとすら思えることがあります。そんな日本人にこちらの大事な仕事を任せて大丈夫なのだろうかと疑問に思うんです。言いたいことをはっきりと、しかも自信をもって表明するというのはビジネスの基本ではありませんか!?

日本人の反論　外国人は日本人の言うことをなかなか理解してくれないだけじゃなく、我々のプレゼンテーションから**とんでもない結論**を導きだしたりするんです。本当に我々の言うことを聞いているんだろうかって思うことがよくあります。お互いに合意したと思って

Japanese people really have to bone up on their presentation skills.

Why is it that the Japanese are so bad at presenting what they want to say? The content of what they say lacks logic, and they seem to have absolutely no confidence. With such poor presentation skills, how are they ever going to persuade anyone to do business with them?

Foreigner's grievance: I'm in charge of sales and was sent to Japan from London. I always tell my Japanese staff to speak clearly when they make their reports, but they don't seem to be able to.

I feel like they're **lacking in logic**. When they give their opinions, I want them to take a logical, rational approach. If a guy can't make clear what he wants to say, with confidence, people are going to wonder whether he has any **get-up-and-go**, whether he really believes what he's saying.

Whenever Japanese people speak, they never seem to have confidence—somehow they always seem nervous and fearful. Occasionally, it's made me wonder, "Is this guy hiding something? Is there something he doesn't want to give away?" It makes you wonder whether it'll be safe to get people like that to take on a job. Surely it's one of the most basic things in business to be clear and forthright, and furthermore to express yourself with confidence.

Japanese retort: Not only do foreigners show little understanding of what we Japanese want to say in our presentations, they also often draw the **most ridiculous conclusions**. Often I find myself wondering whether they've really heard what we've tried to say. And this is even more so when, just when I think we're agreed on something,

いたのに、こちらの予測とまったく違う動きをされたりするから尚更なのです。つまり、あれだけ説明したのに、結局我々が言ったことが理解されてなかったということが日常茶飯事なのです。

　我々は十分に準備してプレゼンテーションをしたつもりですよ。きっと彼らは自分たちのやりたいことや、言いたいことで頭が一杯で、我々の考えを理解しようとはしないんでしょう。こうした問題が続くようでは、とても一緒に仕事はできないですね。

分析

　外国人が日本人のプレゼンテーションをよく理解できない理由の1つに、日本人が物事の背景から説明を始めることが原因であることは、前の項で説明しました。これをもう少し分析するなら、日本人が説明する背景とは、欧米の人にとっては**単なる事例**にすぎないことが多いということです。

　欧米の人は、まず結論、あるいは言いたいことの主旨を述べ、その次にどうしてそういった結論となるのかという理由を解説し、3番目にその理由をサポートするための事例やデータなどを引き合いに出します。そして、最後に全体のまとめをもう一度行い締めくくるのです。日本人が最初に行おうとする背景説明、つまり起承転結の起の部分は、彼らにとっては3番目にあたる事例の1つに過ぎない場合が多いのです。こうした論理構築法の違いによって、欧米の人は日本人は論理的でないというのですが、日本人にとっては極めて論理的な方法でプレゼンテーションを行っているのです。

　この行き違いに**拍車をかける**のが、ジェスチャーが少なく、あ

often a completely unexpected move is made, unrelated to anything we Japanese expected. In other words, so often we'll go to so much trouble to make a speech, and we find that they haven't taken account of the significance of a word of it!

We believe we go to a lot of trouble to make effective presentations. Probably, their heads are simply so full of what they themselves want to do or say, they can't be bothered to try to understand what our intentions are. It's going to be hard to work together if these sorts of problems continue.

Analysis

One reason that foreigners often don't understand Japanese people's presentations is because the Japanese tend to start everything with a background explanation. (This is something we dealt with in the previous case.) But, if I can just add a little more analysis, what Japanese take as background for their explanation, to Westerners often seems little more than a **simple case study**.

Westerners start their presentations with their conclusion, or they make a statement about what they will argue; then, they explain the reasons that they have used to reach that conclusion—and only then do they bring out the case studies or data to support those reasons. They bring the presentation to an end with a summary of the whole argument. Often, the background explanations that the Japanese try to start their arguments with (that is to say, the "Introduction" part of the traditional rhetorical method of "Introduction, Development, Turn, and Conclusion") is assumed by Westerners to be one of a number of case studies that, in their way of thinking, should properly come in the third stage. It's this difference in the logical structure of argumentation that causes Westerners to say that Japanese aren't logical. As far as the Japanese themselves are concerned, however, they are carrying out their presentation in an extremely logical way.

Something that **exacerbates** this misunderstanding is the way

まり表情豊かではないという日本人の特徴です。強い視線と日本人には派手に見えるジェスチャーによって、欧米の人は相手がその提案内容にいかに自信を持っているか、熱心であるかということを無意識のうちに推し量ります。論理構築法の違いと、プレゼンテーションを行うときのボディ・ランゲージの違いが、二者の間の誤解を助長するのです。

　欧米の人は、少なくともジェスチャーなどの外見や、英語の上手下手だけで相手を評価しないよう努めるべきです。そして、日本人は日本人で、相手の文化背景に合わせたスタイルでプレゼンテーションを行うよう、工夫することも必要です。そうした努力がなければ、プレゼンテーションの内容がいくら素晴らしくても、欧米人には日本人の主旨が理解できず、プレゼンテーターのビジネス上の能力にまで**疑問を投げかけて**しまうのです。

ソリューション

❶ なんといっても起承転結法ではなく、最も強調したいポイントから話していくように。ポイントのあとにその理由、そして理由をサポートするいくつかの事例、そして最後に結論とまとめを。

❷ 各論の事例からスピーチをする習慣を改めよう。広島、長崎の話からではなく、「核を廃絶しよう」というメインテーマから話をすべき。広島、長崎は、メインテーマの次に語られる「理由」をサポートする事例なのだ。

❸ 豊かな表情にジェスチャーを交え、フレンドリーに。プレゼンをするあなたはその場をコントロールする権利がある。自信をもって翻弄されずにさばいていこう。決して感情的にならないように。

Japanese are very sparing with their gestures and tend to keep facial expressions to a minimum. Westerners, on the other hand, try to show how certain they are that the proposal they are suggesting is a good one, and how enthusiastic they are about it—getting this subconscious message across by looking at the listeners directly, and with gestures that (to the Japanese) look somewhat overdone. It's these differences in argumentation logic, and in body language used in presentations that widen the gap between the two sides.

Westerners should try to avoid judging the other side merely by their gestures and outward demeanor, or whether or not the other side is fluent in English. The Japanese, too, should try to aim for a presentation style that matches the cultural background of the people to whom they're delivering the presentation. Without such efforts, no matter how impressive the content of the presentation, their good intentions won't get through to the Westerners, and the presentation will end up **casting doubts** as to Japanese skills in the business arena.

Solution

❶ It is important to start with the thing you want to emphasize the most rather than using the "introduction, development, turn, and conclusion" style. After making the point, tell the reason, and then support it with examples. Finally, give the conclusion and summary.

❷ Get into the habit of making speeches with examples of each particular item. Rather than talking about Hiroshima and Nagasaki, get down to the main point and say, "Let's abolish nuclear weapons." Hiroshima and Nagasaki are examples that support the reason which is discussed after your main theme.

❸ Be friendly, making your face expressive and using gestures. You are the one making the presentation, so you are in control. Be confident and deal with things without losing control. Be certain not to get emotional.

日本人は、言葉足らずであいまいだよ。

日本人はあいまいだとよく言われるけどその通りだね。実際、プレゼンテーションをしていても、なぜそのプレゼンテーションをするのかという理由すら、こちらに伝わってこないから困ったものだ。

外国人の不満 私は、アメリカ政府の役人です。日本が担当で、よく日本の官僚のプレゼンを聞いたりします。

実は、よほど注意深く確認を重ねないと、日本人の言っていることを誤解して捉えてしまいます。というのも私からみれば、日本人は**舌足らず**なのです。彼らの言い分を聞いても、彼らの言いたいことは実際の半分もこちらに伝わってこないんです。これは決して英語の問題じゃない。だって、我々の仕事は数字や資料を交換すれば十分に意思疎通ができる性格のものだから。

特にわからないのが、彼らが主張する事柄の理由付け。そして時々それをサポートする実例などが論理的でなかったりする。だから、そこを指摘してもっと説明を引き出そうとするけれど、彼らはますますしどろもどろ。その部分では英語力のハンディキャップに同情しますがね。でもそれならそれで対応の仕方もあるだろうに、ただ黙って立ち往生されたりするから、こちらも「この人本当に仕事のできる人なんだろうか」って思ってしまう。

いったい、日本人のニーズを正確に把握するにはどうすればいいんだろうか?

Japanese aren't explicit enough—they leave everything vague.

Japanese are just as vague as people say they are. During their presentations, for example, we often don't even know why they're doing the presentation. It's really a problem.

Foreigner's grievance: I'm a US government official. I deal with matters related to Japan, so I often hear presentations from Japanese bureaucrats.

The fact of the matter is that even if you repeatedly confirm everything extremely carefully, you'll still misunderstand what Japanese people are saying. It's because, for me, Japanese just **don't explain things well**. No matter how hard you listen, I'd say not even half of what they're trying to say comes across. And it's not just a matter of their English—I mean, with our kind of work, there shouldn't be any problem in communicating what we need to say: all we have to do is give each other the relevant figures and data.

What gets especially difficult to understand is the back-up reasons they give for various circumstances. And sometimes the case studies they present to support their opinions aren't logical. But when we point this out to them, and try to draw out a better explanation, they just flounder even more. To some extent I sympathize, because they're talking in English, not their native language. But there ought to be ways they can deal with that. Instead they just clam up and start getting shifty, so we end up thinking to ourselves, "Does this person know what he's doing at all?"

I just don't know the best way of grasping what Japanese people expect from us.

日本人の反論　いえね、我々はもう十分すぎるくらい説明をしたと思うんですよ。これが重要だ、あのことを先に片づけるべきだとかね。ところが、彼らはすぐにコストがどうなっているとか、予算削減をしなければならないからだめだとか言ってかき回して、こちらに対応しようとはしてくれない。

彼らは**細かいところばかりをつついて**、どんどん本筋からはずれた議論へと動かしていってしまう。ましてこちらは十分な英語力を持っていないので、ますます追いつめられていくんです。でも、我々の主張することは、日本政府のニーズによるものなのです。それだけにもっと我々のことを信じて柔軟に対応してほしいのです。

彼らはこちらの事情を知ろうともしないで、デスクの上の数字だけをつついてくるんですから、困ったものですよ。

分析

　日本には中国からきた「一を聞いて十を知る」という言葉があるように、仕事のできる人であれば、相手の雰囲気や微妙な表現などから相手の真意を読み取るものだという意識があります。小さな島の中で、同じ言語で長年にわたって交流してきた日本人には、確かに相手にすべてのことを言わなくても、メッセージは十分に伝わる部分もあるかもしれません。

　ところが、欧米の人は、そうした日本人のコミュニケーション・スタイルに翻弄されてしまうのです。日本人の「あうんの呼吸」の部分が伝わってこなかったり、日本人なら「そこまで言わなくてもわかってくれるだろう」というところで、日本側の意図が伝達されていなかったということが、よく起こるのです。実は、多言語多文化にもまれながら生きてきた欧米の人にとっては、「**十のことを理路整然と説明して、はじめて十のことを伝えることができる**」というスタンスがビジネスでは常識となっています。

Japanese retort: That's not true. We think the explanations we make are more than adequate. We point out what is important, and which matters need to be dealt with first, etc. But they are so quick to put an oar in, immediately bringing up points like "How much is all this going to cost?" or "We have to decrease the budget"—not taking any notice of what we are trying to say.

They keep on **niggling,** and end up leading the argument far away from where we intended it to go. Especially since we're not talking in our native language, we really feel put under pressure. But the points we are making represent the needs of the Japanese government, and since this is so, we wish they'd believe in us and deal with us flexibly.

It's so hard to deal with them—they don't even try to find out about our situation in Japan, but simply argue looking at the figures on their desks.

Analysis

In Japan there is a saying, originally from China, that you "**listen to one thing, and learn ten**"—meaning that if you're a capable person, you'll be able to read a person's intentions from the atmosphere that surrounds him or her and the person's subtle comments. For Japanese, who for centuries had exchanges in one language on the same small group of islands, there may be some truth in the idea that an understanding of one's partner is possible without having to put everything into words.

Westerners, however, tend to be confused by this kind of Japanese communication style. It often happens that the close, almost unthinking coordination that is presumed upon by the Japanese doesn't transmit well to them. The Japanese rely too much on the idea that what they mean will be understood; that there is no need actually to be explicit. For Westerners, who have lived all their lives in a multilingual and multicultural environment, it is common sense in business that "**if you want ten things understood, you have to say ten things explicitly**."

　したがって、欧米の人は、人がプレゼンテーションをしているとき、わからないところや、理屈の合わないところがあったら、積極的に質問したり指摘したりするのです。「そこの数字のいわんとするところがわからない」とか、「この実例の信頼性はどこに」といった細かい質問をされることも多々あるのです。また、自分がいかに知識を持っているかということをアピールするために質問をする人もいるから大変です。

　このギャップを埋めるには、ちょうど闇の中でお互いに声を掛け合いながら仕事をするかのような地道なコミュニケーションが必要になります。すべてを一度に解決しようとするのではなく、日本人のプレゼンテーションを聞いて理解できなかったことを文章で**箇条書きにして**、日本人にじっくりと考えてもらう時間を与えることも一つの方法でしょう。

　また、日本側も自分の主張の理由をできるだけ明解に述べることができるように、欧米の人が「なぜ?」と尋ねてきそうなところを、事前に補強し準備しておくことも大切です。もちろん、そうした理由をサポートするデータは多ければ多いほど成功します。

　「一を聞いて十を知る」文化と「十を聞いて十を伝える文化」とでは、その差の九がうまく伝わっていない可能性があるということを、真剣に受けとめたいものです。

ソリューション

❶ 一を聞いて十をわかってくれるのは、同じ文化背景に育った日本人の間だけ。一から十まで、どうロジックをもって話していけるかが勝負となる。

❷ 相手がどれくらい理解しているか、常に確認を励行しよう。メモでもメールでも、そして口頭でも。

❸ 海外の人からでそうな質問を、最初に想定して予行演習をしておくことも一案。

Accordingly, when Westerners make presentations, if there is anything they don't understand or that doesn't make logical sense, they make it their business to ask questions and point this out. So they'll often tell you straight, "Without the figures you're not making sense," or else, "What evidence do you have to back up this example?" And things are made even more difficult because there are also some people who ask questions to show off their own ability.

In order to cover this gap, communication at ground level is vital. Imagine that you are working in pitch darkness, and have to call out to let each other know where you are. One method is not to try and solve everything there on the spot, but for the Westerners to **itemize** in a report all the things they couldn't understand when they heard the Japanese side's presentation, and thus give that side enough time to think about what they did wrong.

It's also vital that the people on the Japanese side prepare themselves with back-up arguments so that they can deal with topics it looks as if the other side might query. Of course, the more data you have to support the reasons you have, the better.

When it's a matter of one culture that believes that you "listen to one thing, and learn ten" interacting with another culture that believes that "learning ten things involves having those ten things said clearly," obviously, the former will have to make due allowance for the possibility that as much as nine parts of what they're saying won't come across.

Solution

❶ The idea of "hearing one thing and understanding ten" is something that is shared only by Japanese people because of their common cultural background. The key is to explain the logic of how you got from one to ten.

❷ Be sure to always confirm whether the person understands you or not. You can do it with memos, email, or verbally.

❸ One technique might be to first predict what questions a foreigner could ask and practice responding to them.

ねえ日本人、ベネフィットがなけりゃ やる気なくすよ。

日本人の仕事についての説明や反応を見ていると、本当にこの仕事をやりたいのかどうか疑問に思えてくる。いつも難しい点や、不可能な点ばかりを強調して、解決方法やそのプロジェクトの長所などがぜんぜん見えてこないんだ。

外国人の不満　私はサンフランシスコで健康食品を開発しています。今まで何度も日本での販売を伸ばしたいといろいろ努力してみたのですが、日本側がどうも積極的ではないのです。

　日本人は新しいことにチャレンジすることを嫌がりますね。というより何に対しても消極的で嫌になる。**こちらがどんな提案をしても、**「それは難しいですね」とか、「簡単ではないんですよ。これこれの問題があってね」といったコメントばかり。

　しかも、日本人が何か提案をするときですら、彼らが本当にその**提案を前に進めたい**のかどうかわからなくなる。だって、彼らはリスクばかり強調するから。私は日本人がもっと協力的であってほしいといつも思うんです。そして、できることならばもっと積極的にいろんな提案をしてほしいのです。これって、一緒にビジネスをやっているなら当然期待してもいいことですよね。

日本人の反論　欧米の人は、ともかく急いで物事を進めたがる。それはそれでいいんですが、ときどきあまりにも性急で**十分な準備**ができないまま、走りだそうとしているような気がしてならないのです。彼らはプレゼンテーションはうまいんだけど、実際に仕事を始めてみると往々にしてうまくいかないことが多い。そうなると、ああで

Um, Mr. Japanese, if there's no benefit, we'll lose our motivation.

> Often when a Japanese person is giving an explanation about or a reaction to a project, we find ourselves wondering, "Does this person see any point at all in doing this job?" They put so much emphasis on what is difficult or impossible about a project, and nothing on possible methods for solution, or the benefits.

Foreigner's grievance: I work developing health food products in San Francisco. In the past we've made efforts to improve our sales in Japan many times, but our Japanese partners never seem very positive about it.

Japanese people seem to dislike trying new things. I can't stand the way Japanese are so fearful and negative about things. **Whatever proposal we make**, they come back with "That'll be difficult," or "It's not that simple. There's such-and-such a problem."

Even when it's a proposal that comes from the Japanese themselves, I sometimes wonder whether they are really serious about wanting to **go ahead with** it. All they do is stress the risks! I'm always wishing the Japanese could be more cooperative, and if possible I'd like them to have a more positive attitude and make lots of proposals. Surely this is not too much to expect if one is doing business with someone.

Japanese retort: Westerners put speed before anything else; they want to get on with a job as soon as they can. Okay, that's all well and good—but sometimes they're too impatient, and I just can't help feeling they're off running the race without making **due preparation**. The presentations they make are great, but more often than not, when they actually start on the job, things go wrong. And then all they do

Round 2 I Don't Understand What You're Saying, Japanese People   115

もないこうでもないって言い訳ばかり。だから、最初からちゃんと準備をするべきなんですよ。

　その点、我々は違います。あらゆる人の意見を聞いて、あらゆる角度から検討を重ねた上で、慎重に物事を進めるのです。だから、最初のうちにできるだけいろんな状況に対応できるようじっくりと構えるのは当然のことと言えるのではないですか。

分析

　日本人はまず**リスクを考え**、そのことを強調しながら、あらゆる関係者と打ち合わせ、コンセンサスをとりながら物事を進めていこうとします。このせいでビジネス上のプレゼンテーションでも、ついついリスクを強調するあまり、欧米の人から消極的だという誤解を受けてしまうのです。

　ところが、欧米流のプレゼンテーションでは、プレゼンテーターはまずその案件を実施することのベネフィットや会社や関係者にとってのメリットを強調しようとします。このベネフィットが十分に相手に伝わらず、リスクだけが云々される場合、欧米の人はその案件に対して失望するか、あるいはやる気をそがれてしまいます。聞き手は、プレゼンテーターの出す資料や、論理を検討し、そこに整合性があればあとはアクションプラン（行動計画）について打ち合わせ、実際の行動の中でリスクを検討していこうとします。

　こうした日米間でのプレゼンテーションのあり方の違いが、相手のやる気に対する誤解の原因となるのです。

　誤解を埋めるには、日本側はプレゼンテーションをともかく前向きに、ベネフィットを強調し、そのベネフィットを獲得するた

is make excuses about this or that not being right. That's why it's so important to make due preparations at the very start.

We're quite different in this respect: we take things very slowly, listening to everyone's opinion, and looking at things again and again from every possible angle. Surely it's the obvious thing, to prepare for a project thoroughly at the very early stages so that one is ready from the start to handle whatever circumstances may arise.

Analysis

The Japanese like to proceed in everything they do by first reaching a consensus of opinion, stressing and **mulling over** all the possible **risks**, and holding meetings with all the people involved. Because of this, in business presentations they tend to emphasize the risks far too much and give the mistaken impression to Westerners that they have a negative attitude.

By contrast, in Western presentations the presenter first tries to emphasize the positive benefits that will accrue if the proposal is put into effect, and the advantages for society or for the other people involved. If these benefits are not adequately gotten across to the other party, and if only the risks are stressed, the Westerners will either lose hope in the proposal, or lose all interest and determination to put it into effect. The listeners examine the logic and the data that the presenter gives, and if everything looks to be in agreement, they then have a meeting about the plan of action, and will only deal with the risks when a plan is actually being put into action.

This kind of difference in the way presentations are made in Japan and in Western countries often calls into question the determination of the other person to do the job.

In order to make up for such misunderstandings, the Japanese side should try most of all to be positive in their discussions—to

めにはどのようなリスクを乗り越えなければならないかという論旨で話を進めるようにしたいものです。そして、欧米の人は、物事を達成していくために、まずリスクを考える日本側のアプローチに協力するよう、いろいろなリスクヘッジに関する提案を日本人に対して行ってみることをお薦めします。

そしてできれば、そうした提案を公式な打ち合わせの前後に、もっとプライベートな場をもうけ、リラックスした雰囲気の中で行うと効果的でしょう。

ソリューション

❶ リスクや否定的な会話から入るのは厳に慎もう。彼らは日本人と違って、それを拒絶、消極性と誤解してしまう。慎重にいきたいが故の否定的な会話が全てを台無しにしてしまう。

❷ ベネフィット、メリットをまず強調し、それを実現するには何を乗り越えなければならないかという論法が、ビジネス・ディスカッションやプレゼンテーションの基本となる。

❸ リスクを回避し、目標を達成するためのアクションプランがあれば、さらに効果的。

put the emphasis in their argument on the benefits, even though in order to reap those benefits there will be some risks to overcome. And I recommend that Westerners help matters along by showing their willingness to cooperate with the Japanese approach to carefully weigh the risks in a project, by making various suggestions about ways to hedge the risks.

And if you can, try to arrange a rather more private meeting in a relaxed atmosphere around the time of the formal discussion regarding a proposal.

Solution

❶ One should refrain from entering into conversations about risk or negative things. Unlike Japanese people, foreigners object to this sort of thing, and may mistake it for negativity. Talking negatively about something that you want done carefully may completely ruin it.

❷ A fundamental of business discussions and presentations is using a line of reasoning in which one emphasizes the benefits and merits first, and then explains what has to be overcome in order to realize them.

❸ It can be more effective to have a plan of action for avoiding risk and achieving a goal.

事例

13

ブレインストーミングなんだから
日本人も参加してよ!!

日本人はプレゼンテーションなどの場で、何か問題が起きたり、問題点を
指摘されたりすると、ただそこで立ち往生してしまう。我々とざっくばら
んに意見交換して、どうして前向きに物事を解決しようとしないんだろう。

外国人の不満　実は、日本人のプレゼンテーションは単に論理的じゃ
ないだけではない。彼らの態度には、我々と仕事をしようというス
タンスがまったく見えず、そこに大きな不満があるんです。

　私は、医療技術の交流のために、ある日本の医大に滞在しています。
私が一番いやなのは、プレゼンテーションのやり方がわかりにくい
ことではないんです。それは慣れれば解決できます。問題は、一緒
に物事を解決しようとしない彼らの対応なのです。

　日本人はなぜ話し合いをしているのに1人で黙り込んだり、日本人
だけでこそこそと話し込んだりするのでしょうか。より多くの人と
意見交換して、よりよいアイデアを導き出すのは、ビジネスをする
上での「いろはのい」じゃないかって思うんですが。

　彼らは我々のことを信頼していないのでしょうか。それとも、と
ても**自惚れ**ていて、何でも自分たちだけでできるとでも思っている
のでしょうか。そこで、たまりかねてこちらから何かアイデアを出
すと、それはあたかもブラックホールの中に投げ込まれたボールの
ように、彼らからは何の反応も返ってこない。

　こんなことで、今後もずっと彼らと一緒に仕事ができるかどうか、
とても不安です。どうすれば、日本人はもっと心を開いてくれるの
でしょうか?

日本人の反論　ともかく彼らはうるさいんです。こっちがじっくりと

It's brainstorming, so Japanese people have to participate too!

> In presentations and so on, whenever a problem arises or someone points out a fault in their argument, the Japanese just act shifty. Why don't they exchange opinions with us in as frank and straightforward a way as possible?

Foreigner's grievance: The Japanese don't just totally lack logic in the way they make their presentations; it's their stance that really gets to me—it totally lacks a spirit of cooperation.

I'm at a Japanese medical school as part of a medical technology exchange program. The thing that bothers me the most isn't that the presentations are hard to follow. If you get used to it, it doesn't bother you. The problem is that the Japanese don't try to work with us to resolve things.

Why is it that even though everyone is discussing things together, some Japanese people will just stay silent, and others will have whispered discussions with the other Japanese people? Surely it's one of the first things you learn in the field of business that you try and draw out good ideas by exchanging opinions with as many people as possible.

Is it that they don't trust us? Or are they just so **conceited** that they think they can handle everything fine themselves? Then, when we brainstorm and bring out some idea, it's just as if we've thrown a ball into a black hole in space—not a word comes back from them.

I really worry how much longer I can work with them if this is how things are going to be. What's the best way of getting Japanese to open up?

Japanese retort: Those guys are so irritatingly impatient! We're

考えて対応しようとしているのに、横からああでもない、こうでもないって割り込んできて。しかも、その主張が結構ゴリ押しで、ただ自分たちの意見を押しつけようとしているとしか思えない。実際、紆余曲折のあとで、最終的には彼らの意見や方針通りになってしまうケースも多いのです。そんなとき、我々は「ああ、あれこれ言っても、結局彼らは自分たちの考え方が一番で、日本人にはただそれに従ってほしいんだ」って思ってしまいます。

彼らももっと**謙虚**に物事を学ぶ姿勢をもってほしいものです。時間をかけてじっくりと打ち合わせ、お互いのことを理解して、さらにより深くいろいろな要素を考えながらアイデアを練り上げるようにしてもらいたいものです。これこそ、ビジネスの「いろはのい」ですよね。

分析

日本人と欧米人とのコミュニケーション・スタイルのもっとも際立った違いは、ブレインストーミングという概念があるかないかです。

前章の事例7でも解説したように、欧米の人はプレゼンテーションの最中や会話の中で、何か困難な状況に直面した場合、比較的カジュアルにお互いに意見を出し合って、よりよい結論を導き出そうとします。自らが積極的に意見を披露することをよしとする文化背景を持つ彼らは、その場に立場の高い人がいれば、さらに強く自己のアイデアをPRしてくるかもしれません。

対照的に、日本人は自らの意見をプレゼンテーションすることに対して、**慎重**です。特にその場に上司が同席している場合、上下

trying to give full consideration to how we ought to handle a matter, and here they come and interfere, with comments and criticisms. And they make their assertions in such an **overbearing manner**, it seems like all they're interested in is getting their own opinion across. In fact, things often end up with them going ahead in accordance with their own opinions and policies anyway, even after all the troubles and difficulties. And then we think, "See, they make a pretense of asking for our opinion, but they were going to go their own way anyway, and all they want is for the Japanese to comply with them and follow along."

It would be good if they were more **humble**—less arrogant in the way they go about things. How nice it would be if they took the time to hold meetings in order to think about matters properly and to understand everybody's point of view, and then considered the various elements—and developed ideas this way. For us, this is one of the basic things you have to learn if you want to do good business.

Analysis

One of the most outstanding differences in communication styles between Japanese and Westerners lies in the ideas surrounding the concept of brainstorming.

As I explained in my commentary in Case 7 of the previous chapter, when Westerners encounter something they have difficulty with in the middle of a presentation or during a conversation, they will ask for each other's opinions relatively casually, and try to lead the argument forward to a more suitable conclusion. Since they come from a culture where it is considered a good thing to reveal one's own opinion in a positive, assertive way, perhaps especially if someone of high status happens to be around, they will try to promote their own ideas particularly strongly.

By contrast, the Japanese are highly **circumspect** with regard to giving a presentation with their own opinions. Especially when one of their senior colleagues is present at the same meeting, out of deference

関係への配慮から部下は得てして**雄弁**になることを控えます。また、小さい頃から、じっくりと黙って考えることが美徳であるという教育を受けてきた日本人は、欧米人のように気軽にアイデアをテーブルの上に投げて討議する方法を軽率な行為と考えがちです。

したがって、こうした場に遭遇すると、日本人はより**寡黙**になり、欧米の人が雄弁になるせいで、欧米の人の意見で場が埋め尽くされてしまう状況になってしまうこともあるのです。このように、意見をテーブルの上に出し合って、それを叩き合い、より高度な結論を導きだそうとする行為をブレインストーミングといいますが、この概念自体、日本人には縁遠いものだということを、双方とも知っておくべきです。

すでに何度か解説したように、例えば、お酒の席とか、カジュアルな食事の席などでは、日本人は比較的オープンに意見交換をします。そうした意見交換の場を持つには、まず人間関係を構築しなければなりません。欧米の人が日本人と仕事をするときには、単に会議の席だけではなく、幅広い機会を利用して情報を収集するよう努めてもらいたいものです。

ソリューション

❶ 海外の人たちと仕事を進めるには、ブレインストーミングの方法を習得すべし。会話の中で意見を戦わせながら、よりよい解決方法を見いだしていく彼らのやり方は、じっくり腰を据えて考えようとする日本人には苦手なテクニック。

❷ ブレインストーミングの場では、意見を表明することに意義がある。一人で解決しようとせずに、意見を表明して皆でそれをたたきながら向上させる。正解は、皆と一緒に導くのだ。

❸ それでも、公式な場所でのブレインストーミングが苦手ならば、日本流に場を変えて、食事やお酒の場に誘ってカジュアルに。そこから少しずつブレインストーミングのテクニックを習得しよう。

to their relative positions the junior colleague will most often refrain from becoming too **talkative**. Moreover, since Japanese people have been raised from childhood to believe that being quiet and thinking over a situation carefully is a virtue, they tend to consider a method of discussion where one just throws ideas onto the table in a casual manner as rather reckless behavior.

Accordingly, when they encounter this kind of situation, Japanese people become even more **reticent**—and since the Westerners then get even more talkative, it often happens that the discussion becomes completely one-sided. Throwing one's ideas and thoughts out onto the table just as they occur like this is what is called brainstorming. But the very concept of brainstorming is one that means little to the Japanese—this is a fact of which both sides should be aware.

As I've already explained several times, Japanese exchange opinions relatively openly in casual situations, over a drink or a meal. In order to have that kind of exchange, relations between the parties have to be built up. Westerners would do well when they work with Japanese to make use of a variety of opportunities to find out more about what the other side thinks—and not just rely on formal meetings and conferences.

Solution

❶ You should acquire the ability to brainstorm when working with foreigners. Their method is looking for a better solution by trading various viewpoints during the conversation. It is a technique that Japanese, who consider things slowly before speaking, are not fond of.

❷ In a brainstorming session, expressing an opinion itself is meaningful. Do not try to solve problems alone. Express your opinions, and let everyone improve them by mincing things out. The correct answer will be found by working together.

❸ However, if you do not like brainstorming in public, follow the Japanese way of changing the venue to a casual one where it can be done over a meal or drinks. From there, you can gradually start to acquire the ability to brainstorm.

どうして日本人は感情や感傷で
ビジネスをすすめるの？

日本人はビジネスをしているのか、友人と遊んでいるのかわからないときがある。論理的な展開が必要なところで、妙に感情的になったり、感傷にとらわれて判断をしたり。彼らの行動は本当に不可解だ。

外国人の不満　私はフランスの自動車会社から派遣され日本の支社に勤務しています。最近日本の販売ネットワークを見直し、**効率化しようとも**ちかけたら、とても感情的な反発を受け、戸惑ってしまいました。

　よくあることなんだけど、こちらが論理的に物事を指摘したり、反論したりすればするほど、日本人は感情的に対応しようとするんです。これでは、議論が続けられないですよね。あるときなんか、こちらはともかくロジックに従って判断しようとしているのに、これだけ熱心に準備したんだからいいじゃないかなんて日本側に言われて、対応に困ったことがありました。

　いえね、熱心であることはいいことだけど、結果が伴わなければ意味ないでしょう。厳しいビジネスの場で感傷にとらわれてばかりいることはできないことを、日本人だって十分に理解しているはずなのに……。

Why do Japanese do business in such an emotional, sentimental way?

> Sometimes I don't know whether Japanese people think they're doing business or spending time with friends. Just when it's necessary for logical deployment, they get strangely emotional and make judgments based on sentimentality. I really don't understand their behavior.

Foreigner's grievance: I work for a French automaker. I was dispatched to work in the Japanese branch office. Recently, when we reviewed the Japanese sales network and made proposals for **streamlining things**, we were bewildered by the very emotional negative reactions we received.

It often happens that the more logically we criticize something or make an argument against one of their suggestions, the more the Japanese react in an emotional, irrational way. There's no way we can have a discussion like that, is there? And sometimes, when we try to make a judgment along logical lines, the Japanese side remonstrates with us, saying "What do you mean? We've put so much energy and enthusiasm into preparing this, can't you let it go?" or some such thing, and we don't know what to say.

Okay, well it's great that they put so much energy into a project, but if the results don't match up, it's meaningless, isn't it? I would have thought that even the Japanese would understand that it's a tough world out there in the marketplace, and you can't get taken over by emotions.

日本人の反論　ともかく、英語ですべてを表現するのは我々にとっては至難のわざですよね。しかも、長い伝統と様々な繊細な人間関係によって成り立っている日本のビジネス環境を彼らに理解してもらうのは大変です。それなのに、彼らは我々のそうした努力に敬意を払おうとはせずに、ただ非合理的だと一刀両断で自分たちの論旨で**押し切ろう**とする。だからそうじゃないんだと必死になって英語で説明しようとしても、「なぜ? それはおかしいでしょ」と言って我々の言うことを最後まで聞こうともしないんです。

　例えば取引先によっては、商品の納入を決めるまで長い時間をかけ、そのあとで我々に試験的に小さな注文を出してみたりしますよね。もちろん、将来のチャンスに向けて、我々はそれがどんなに小さな注文でも、熱心に対応しなければなりません。時には、業界でよりスムーズに活動できるようにするために、十分な利益があがらなくても、おつき合いでビジネスをしなければならないときだってあるでしょう。でも、彼らはそうした事情は理解せず、ただ数字だけで判断し、そんな小さな注文のためにコストをかける必要はないと断定します。**目先のことを言えば**、それは確かに論理的かも知れません。でも、長期的展望に立てば、我々の行動がいかに論理的であるか、理解してほしいものです。

分析

　日本人が国内のマーケットでどれだけ苦労して市場を広げているかは、欧米の人にはなかなか理解してもらえません。しかも、そんなとき、日本人はたどたどしい英語で、自分たちがいかに苦労をしているか、そして日本のマーケットがいかに複雑かという

Japanese retort: Well, first of all, consider what an extremely difficult task it is for us to have to say everything we need to in English. And it's also *very* difficult to get foreigners to understand the business environment in Japan, which rests on long traditions and delicate relations. Despite this, they pay no attention to the efforts we're making to explain, and claim simply that we're illogical—and they just **bulldoze through** whatever argument it is that they're making. We then become all the more desperate, and do our best to explain that it won't work, but they don't bother to hear us out and just say, "Why? You guys must have a problem!"

For example, sometimes some of our Japanese clients take time to decide whether they will place orders with us, and first try us out, making small orders of goods to find out what we're like. Of course, we respond enthusiastically to any order, no matter how small it may be, in the hope that it will eventually develop into something bigger later. Sometimes, in order to develop business smoothly, one has to make deals for the purpose of developing relationships, even if the accruing profits from these transactions don't amount to much. But Westerners don't understand these things and simply make judgments according to the figures—and they conclude that there's no need to lay out costs for such small orders. **From their short-sighted point of view**, this may be logical; but we'd like them to understand just how logical our actions are in the longer term.

Analysis

It's very difficult to get Westerners to understand just how much trouble the Japanese will have gone to in their efforts to gain a wider share of the domestic market. Furthermore, at these times a Japanese will try to explain in faltering English, emphasizing just how much effort they have made, and just how complex the Japanese market

ことだけを強調してしまうために、欧米の人の熱意をさらに削いでしまうという**悪循環**を生み出してしまいがちです。

　そうしたとき、ついつい限られた英語の語彙や表現方法、さらにはプレゼンテーションの方法の文化的な違いから、日本側はより感情や感傷に訴えてしまいます。それが、欧米の人から見れば、冷静にそして論理的に物事を説明できない日本人への不信感へと発展します。

　この悪循環を防ぐには、まず日本側はビジネスの過去、現在、未来それぞれを的確に表現できる数字や表などを用意することが必要です。特に将来の予測を強調し、そのために現在は投資しているのだという発想でプレゼンテーションを行いたいものです。

　そして、欧米から来た人々は、日本人担当者が過去にどのような実績をもつ人かを注意深く検討し、国内で実績を上げている人であれば、まずはその人材を信用して予算を与え、仕事を任せてみるスタンスをとることも大切です。単に自分の考えを伝えるのではなく、数字や未来の予測といった共通の言語となり得る資料や表をもって、日本側の主張を最後まで聴いた上で、協力的な質問をするよう心がけたいものです。

　欧米人の中には、質問をすることによって、自らがいかにその分野に精通しているかをPRしようとする人がいますが、異なるビジネス文化で仕事をする以上、そうした対応は慎みましょう。日本のマーケットについて学ぶ**姿勢**をとり、具体的に「教えてもらう」というモードで質問をすることが必要です。

　日本人は、相手が学ぶ姿勢をもっていると理解すれば、心を開きます。態度やビジネスに対する姿勢が、即座の結果やロジック

is—and all this does make the Westerners even less enthusiastic to work with them. A **vicious circle** ensues.

At these times, because of their poor facility with English vocabulary and turns of phrase, and also because of cultural differences surrounding presentation methods, the Japanese side will resort to making appeals to emotion and sentiment. And this will simply lead the Americans to distrust the Japanese, who will be seen as being unable to make explanations in a calm, logical manner.

In order to avoid this vicious circle, the Japanese side should first of all adequately prepare themselves with figures and tables that can give an accurate rendering of the past, present, and future facts surrounding the work at hand. I particularly recommend that when they give presentations, they should make their argument follow a line of predictions for the future, showing that this is why present investments are being made.

Secondly, people who come from the United States and Europe to do business in Japan should make a careful examination of the past record of achievements of the Japanese with whom they are dealing. If this is someone who does have a record of achievement in Japan, it's important to adopt a stance of trusting their ability and entrusting budget matters to them. And it's not just a matter of getting your own opinion across: after listening to what the Japanese side has to say until the very end, you might, using data and tables (surely these are a common language which you can use to discuss figures and future estimates) show how you wish to cooperate, by asking questions.

Some Westerners like to use questions to do a bit of self-promotion and show off how well-informed they are about a particular field. But if you want to do business in a culture that is different from your own, this is something you should refrain from doing. **Adopt a position of** trying to learn about the markets in Japan: it's helpful to ask questions in a way that suggests that you would like the other person to explain matters to you.

Once the Japanese understands that you are willing to learn, he or she will open himself up to you. You should know that one's attitude and stance regarding work possess much more power to move

より日本人の心を動かす原動力になるということを知っておきましょう。努力や真摯な対応が結果以上に重視されることがあるというのも、日本のビジネス文化の特徴なのです。

ソリューション

❶ 確かに英語で複雑な日本のビジネスの背景を説明することは難しい。でも、それなら、相手に時間をかけ、しつこく、じっくりと挑んでいこう。感情や感傷で話をすることは、むしろ逆効果になってしまう。

❷ 未来をどう創るかというスタンスを中心に、過去から現在までの状況を説明しよう。今までの経験だけを強調し、相手の意見を否定しては、国際間のビジネスは進捗しない。

❸ 単に自分のパワーをみせるのではなく、日本人には学ぶ姿勢でアプローチせよと、事前にオリエンテーションをしておくことが肝要。

and affect the Japanese than whether one can show immediate and obvious results, or any logic. It's a particular characteristic of Japanese business culture to attach more importance to the efforts a person makes and the seriousness of his or her manner of dealing with things than results.

Solution

❶ It is difficult to explain the complicated business situation in Japan to someone in English. However, in that case, spend time making an effort to explain things slowly to the person. Emotion and sentiment when speaking can backfire.

❷ Explain the situation from past to present, focusing on the approach of explaining what kind of future it will produce. Just emphasizing your experience, or being negative about another person's opinion is not the way business is carried out internationally.

❸ It can be very important to have an orientation session beforehand, explaining that foreigners should adopt an attitude that is receptive to learning from Japanese, rather than showing off their abilities.

日本人は本気で謝ってるの？
謝るなら結果をだしてよ！

> 日本人は何でもすぐに謝ると言われるが、彼らは本当に自分がまずかっ
> たと思っているのだろうか？ あれは単なる社交儀礼のような気がしてな
> らないんだが。

外国人の不満　私はシカゴに住む食品会社の幹部です。ビジネスで毎
年日本に出張します。例えば、日本で飛行機やホテルを利用したり
するとき、ちょっとしたことで、日本人は「申し訳ありません」って
いうんです。最初は気にしなかったんですが、だんだんと、彼らは
本当に自分が悪かったと思っているのかって疑い始めました。

　というのも、謝った矢先に、結局日本人は同じ事を繰り返したり、
平気で自分のやりかたを押し通したりすることがあるんですよ。

　いつだったか、ある日本人が「申し訳ありません」っていうから、
何について申し訳ないのか聞いてみたことがあるんです。すると、「い
え特別には……」って言うではないですか。また、あるときなんて、
「申し訳ありません」って言われたあと、「いえ、いいですよ、気にし
ないで」と言うと、何と彼は不服そうに憮然としたんです。これには
戸惑いました。日本人は率直に感情を表明しないって言うけど、こ
のときは本当にそうなんだなあって実感してしまいましたね。

日本人の反論　我々からみれば、欧米の人は逆に全然謝らない。一言
申し訳ないって言ってくれれば済むものを、ああでもないこうでも
ないって言い訳ばかり。別にこっちだって相手を追いつめようとし
ているわけではないのに、やたらとむきになって自分を正当化しよ

Are the Japanese really sincere when they apologize? If you're really sorry, do something about it!

It's often said that the Japanese always apologize about everything. But do they really think they've done anything wrong? I can't help feeling the apologizing is more a matter of form, just empty phrases.

Foreigner's grievance: I'm an executive at a food company in Chicago. I make business trips to Japan every year. For example, when I fly or stay at a hotel, Japanese people always say, "I'm terribly sorry" **over really little things**. At first I didn't mind it, but gradually, I began to get suspicious about whether they really did think they had done something bad.

Because often, as soon as they've apologized, they will go and do the exact same thing again, or brazenly just **carry on** with what they were doing in the first place.

One time, I actually asked a Japanese man who had apologized in this way what he was apologizing for. And you know, all he could say in reply was "Oh, nothing in particular!" Another time, when I found myself being apologized to, I answered by saying, "Oh, that's all right, please don't worry about it," and the guy who had apologized looked quite displeased and astonished. It was bewildering. It's often said that the Japanese don't express themselves frankly, and that time I could really see the truth of this.

Japanese retort: From our point of view, people in the West are quite the opposite and don't apologize at all. Sometimes all it needs is a simple apology and the matter would be over, but all they do is keep on making excuses. I can't stand it the way, even when we're not particularly getting on their case about anything, they **get so**

うとするからたまりません。

　特に驚かされるのは、こちらがサービスを受ける**立場**で、相手がこちらに不便をかけたにもかかわらず謝罪の一言もないときです。**ひどいときには**、「これは私の責任ではありません、あっちの部門の問題ですから」なんて言われることもあるんです。彼らの非常識には**閉口させられます**。あそこまで自己主張されると、かえってその人格を疑ってしまいますよね。

分析

　「申し訳ありません」という表現は、日本人がコミュニケーションを行う上で、その場をなごませるための一つの**社交手段**に他なりません。その場に発生した不便や迷惑、あるいは不可解な状況などに対して、相手に向かって「申し訳ありません」と言えば、ほとんどの場合、相手も「いえ、こちらこそ」と応対してきます。これは、お互いに謝り合うことによって、双方の心をなごませ、その後の対話を円滑に進めようとする日本人の知恵であり、常識なのです。

　しかし、これはあくまでも、日本特有のコミュニケーションスタイルであることを、ここで強調しておきます。自らの立場を明解に表現することによって、相手に自らの意志を伝えることをよしとする欧米の人からみれば、この日本人のスタイルは**まどろっこしい**ばかりか、問題の所在を曖昧にしてしまう不可解な行動ともとられかねません。

　もちろん、欧米の人も明らかに自分に非があるときは、謝るものです。ただ、彼らはその場をやわらげる手段として「申し訳ありません」とは言わないのです。そこにたとえ上下関係や、サービスをする側、受ける側といった立場の違いがあっても、相手と**対等**

self-righteous and try to justify themselves.

What really shocks us is when we are **in the position of** customer and thus in a position to be receiving their service—and they do something that causes us inconvenience, and not a single word of apology is offered! **In the worst case**, we'll actually be told by them, "It's not our fault. This is the responsibility of another section." Such rude, irresponsible behavior **puts** us **at a loss for words**. If a person is going to be that rude, well, we tend to wonder about their character.

Analysis

The expression "I'm sorry" (*Mōshiwake arimasen*; literally, "I have no excuses") is in fact just a **social tool** used to soften the mood in situations when Japanese people are communicating with each other. If a person apologizes to other people with these words, which acknowledge the inconvenience and trouble that arise in certain situations, or the difficult circumstances, in nearly every case the other person will respond by saying "No, no, I should apologize to you." By apologizing to each other like this, the two parties are producing a harmonious frame of mind in the other person, and allowing the dialogue to continue smoothly afterwards. Such things constitute practical wisdom and common sense for the Japanese.

But I should emphasize here that this is a communication style that is highly particular to Japan. For Westerners, who regard it as a good thing to let the other person know of one's own thoughts by clearly expressing one's own position, this Japanese way of doing things is not only slow—it can also seem **incomprehensible**, a way of covering up in ambiguity whatever the real problem is.

Of course, Westerners apologize too when it is obvious that the fault is theirs. But they don't use "I'm sorry" as a means of softening the mood of a situation. This is because for a Westerner, it is common sense to try to express oneself **on an equal footing** with one's counterpart, regardless of differences in station, seniority, or whether

に自らの考えを表明しようとするのは、彼らの常識でもあるのです。

　日本人と交流する欧米人は、「申し訳ありません」ということは、何も自分の非を全面的に認めることを意味しないのだということを知っておくべきで、相手への**思いやりの表現**として、日本人は頻繁にそのように言っていることを理解してください。そして、日本人は、欧米の人々が、「申し訳ありません」と言わずに、自らのスタンスを表明してきた場合、それに腹を立てず、じっと相手の言い分に耳を傾け、必要ならば論理的に相手の過ちを指摘したり、解決策を提案したりといった柔軟性をもつことが必要です。

　論理的に物事を解決しようとする欧米流のビジネス文化と、曖昧な中から次第にお互いの接点を見極め、物事を前に進めていこうとする日本流のスタイルとの違いが、「申し訳ありません」という表現をめぐる誤解の背景にはあるのです。

ソリューション

❶ 謝るときは、実際に何について謝っているのか明快にしよう。ただ、その場をつくろい、和らげるための日本流のお詫びは誤解のもと。

❷ もし、相手と行き違いがあった場合は、謝るのではなく、I think we have misunderstanding. というのが効果的。お互いの誤解の原因をといて、未来につなげるスタンスをもとう。

❸ 相手が謝らなくても腹をたてるな。じっくりと相手の言い分を聞いて、あたかも契約をするように、同じ問題が繰り返されないように話し合おう。

one is receiving or giving the services.

Westerners who want to associate with Japanese should know that the words *Mōshiwake arimasen* ("I'm terribly sorry") are used frequently by Japanese people—and they don't necessarily mean that the speaker is acknowledging he or she is completely at fault, but, rather, are used as an **expression of consideration** for the other person. And the Japanese for their part should aim for a bit more flexibility: don't get irritated when Westerners don't apologize and start to explain their own point of view to you; let them finish, and if necessary point out where they are at fault in a logical manner, suggesting ways of solving the problem.

Part of the reason for the misunderstandings that arise around the expression *Mōshiwake arimasen* lies in the difference between the particular business culture that has arisen in the West, where problems are solved logically and rationally, and the Japanese style of doing things, where matters are kept vague and are gradually taken forward by distinguishing a point where the two sides can come together.

Solution

❶ When apologizing, make it clear exactly what you are apologizing for. The Japanese style of apologies for smoothing over problems and relieving tension creates misunderstandings.

❷ If you have a misunderstanding with someone, do not just apologize. It is more effective to say, "I think we have a misunderstanding." Find the cause of the misunderstanding together to improve the relationship for the future.

❸ Even if someone else does not apologize, do not get angry. Listen to the person's point carefully, and discuss it as thoroughly as if it were a contract in order to prevent the problem from reoccurring in the future.

外国人と一緒に
働けない日本人

ROUND **3**

**The Problems Japanese Have
Working with Foreigners**

日本人の上司にお願い。
僕のことを評価してよ。頼むから。

> 日本人はなんでほめてくれないんだろう。「これは難しい」とか、「まだまだ、もっと頑張れ」だとか、すべてが否定的でこちらのやる気をそぐことばかりなんだ。

外国人の不満 僕はオハイオ州にある日系企業に勤めています。僕の上司は日本人。彼は仕事はできて、英語もうまい。でも彼のことでどうしても受け入れられないことがあるんだ。それは、僕が何を言っても否定的にしか反応しないこと。

僕は僕なりにいろいろと準備して、慎重に調査をして意見をいうし、提案をする。ところが、彼はいつでも「もっとしっかり頑張らないと、これじゃあだめだ」とか、「もう1回やり直し。もっとじっくり考えてみろ」などと言って突き放す。これじゃあ、ただ僕の仕事が否定されているだけで、どのように改善してほしいのか何も見えてこない。

具体的な指導は何もせずに、ただ否定的なものの言い方ばかりする彼には、正直なところうんざりしている。きっと彼は僕のことを認めていないんだろうと思うよ。もしかしたら、どうでもいいって思っているんじゃないだろうか。僕自身のキャリアを考えれば、自分のことを評価してくれない上司のもとに勤めていてもしようがない。

せめて、的確な指導を受けられればまだしも、あんなあいまいな表現で否定だけされていると、どうしていいかわからなくなるんだ。もう少し僕のよいところも認めてほしいものだ。

Japanese boss, *please* give me some praise.

Why do the Japanese never give a person any praise? Everything is negative, making you want to give up—either, "This job is difficult to do right," or "You're not there yet, try harder."

Foreigner's grievance: I work for a Japanese company located in Ohio. My superior at work is Japanese. He's good at the job, and his English is great, but there's something about him that really bugs me: whatever I say, he only reacts negatively.

I give opinions and make proposals after thinking about things and conducting tests with the requisite amount of consideration and experimentation, but all he ever does is brush my proposals aside with "No good! You've got to do better than this," or "Think things over a little more, and rewrite this proposal." All I get is denials that my work is any good, and no concrete comments about how I could actually try to make improvements.

Honestly, I've had it up to here with the unhelpful, negative things he says—the lack of any **solid guidance**. I suspect he thinks I have no ability at all. Or maybe he thinks it doesn't matter one way or the other. As far as my career is concerned, it's pointless working for a superior who doesn't value my work.

If I could at least get some precise instruction it would be okay, but when I just get told that what I do isn't good enough, in that generalized way, I have no idea what I should do. I wish he would acknowledge my good points at least.

日本人の反論 「鉄は熱いうちに打て」という言葉があるように、部下が優秀なら、しっかりと指導して、厳しい評価をするのはあたりまえじゃないですか。愛の鞭ってやつですよ（編註：英語では「かわいい子には旅をさせよ」ということわざに訳しています）。部下に育ってもらいたければ、しっかり注意して指導するのは上司として当然の義務でしょう。

　ちやほやしていては、よい人材は育ちませんよ。よく、叱られなくなったらおしまいだって言われるように、部下は可愛いから叱るんです。そのとき手とり足とり指導するはずないでしょ。自分の力で苦労して習得したものこそ、価値あるものなんですから。だから、あえてもう一度しっかり考えて見なさいと言って突き返すんです。

　時間はかかりますが、みんなそうやって苦労して仕事を覚えるんです。そうすれば、単に知識だけではなく、しっかりとノウハウが身につくわけです。外国人は**忍耐力**がなさすぎるんですよ。こちらがよかれと思って言っていることを全部悪意にとって、文句を言うんだから困ったものです。

Japanese retort: You know the saying "Strike while the iron is hot." Well, in the same way, the more talented the people working under you are, the stricter and more demanding you have to be as their superior in their training and evaluation. "Spare the rod and spoil the child" is another saying. Telling one's subordinates what they're doing wrong is one of the duties of a superior, if he wants them to get better at the job.

If all you do is **coddle** your subordinates, they're never going to develop to their full potential. People in Japan say that when nobody bothers to scold you, that's the end. It's because I care for the people working under me that I scold them. Surely I don't need to hold their hands and explain everything to them in detail. The people who are really worth something are the ones who've gained what they've gained through their own efforts. This is why I refuse to accept their ideas immediately, and tell them to think a little harder about whatever they're doing and make it better.

It is time consuming, but this is the way people learn how to do their jobs. This way, they acquire the "knowhow" themselves, and it doesn't remain on a merely conceptual level. Foreigners lack **perseverance**. It's a real problem the way they take everything I say negatively, despite my good intentions. All they do is complain.

分析

　部下をほめることによって、部下にやる気をだしてもらう方法に戸惑う上司が、日本には多いようです。

　事例4を思い出しましょう。そこに書かれているように、フィードバックの手法を習得することが、日本人の上司には**必要不可欠**です。

　まず相手のよいところをほめ、次に相手に質問し、困難だったところの克服方法を話し合い、できるだけ具体的なアドバイスをしながら、最後に相手と仕事の質を高め合うよう改善点を確認するという話し合いのプロセスこそが、フィードバックの手順なのです。つまり、ほめっぱなしでもしかりっぱなしでもまずいのです。

　実際、人の指導の仕方には、日本と欧米、特にアメリカとでは大きな違いがあります。人と人とが長い時間をかけて知り合い、信頼関係の中で、ちょうど**徒弟制度**のような発想で部下を育てようとする日本人と、業務そのものに集中して、その技能の向上のみに焦点をあて部下を指導しようとするアメリカ人とでは、部下に対するアプローチそのものに隔たりがあるのです。

　それは、人材を育成するという言葉があるように、人を育てようというスタンスをとる日本人と、その人の技能を評価し、契約して仕事をしようという欧米の人との違いでもあります。

　したがって、日本では上司は部下にじっくりと向き合い、敢えて試練を与えながら部下の成長を見つめていきます。人を育てるという観点から、部下の全人格的な部分にも関わりながら指導するわけです。その場合、すぐに技能の向上を期待するのではなく、

Analysis

There are a lot of bosses in Japan who are at a loss as to how to motivate their subordinates by praising them.

Let's look back at Case 4. As it said, acquiring the ability to give feedback to subordinates is **indispensable** for Japanese supervisors.

First, you should praise the person. Then, ask him or her questions, discuss how to overcome the problems together, and finally talk with the worker to confirm what needs to be improved on to increase the quality of his or her work, while giving advice that is as specific as possible. This is the feedback procedure. In other words, neither constant scolding nor constant praising is good.

In practice, a huge difference exists in the way Japanese and Westerners (particularly Americans) view guidance and instruction. The difference amounts basically to a gap in the approach adopted by superiors to subordinates in Japan and the United States. The Japanese tend to think that superiors should give training to their subordinates, in something like an **apprenticeship system**—the superior trains the subordinate person-to-person over the course of time, and a relationship of trust develops between them. Americans, on the other hand, put the emphasis on the job, and think that superiors should instruct their subordinates solely with a view to improving their skills and ability.

For the Japanese the emphasis is on helping the person to grow into the job, as is suggested by the phrase *jinzai o ikusei suru*, or "fostering a person of talent." Americans hire a person on the strength of his or her ability to do the job in the first place.

Accordingly, in Japan superiors keep a sharp eye on the progress of their subordinates, putting them through a very thorough, demanding training. They direct them in a way that relates to the total person, and precisely because of this they don't expect immediate improvements in their skills and abilities. Rather, they hope that by

むしろ相手の未熟な部分を指摘し、改善する過程でプロとしての
テクニックを習得していくことを、上司は部下に期待します。

　日本には、上司のやり方を盗めという言葉があります。部下は、
じっくりと年月をかけて、上司の行動や仕事へのアプローチの仕
方を見ながら、そのスキルを次第に自分のものにしていくのです。
　こうした日本的なアプローチを多くの欧米の人はなかなか理解
できないどころか、時には大きな誤解の因となり、雇用関係その
ものにひびがはいることもあるのです。

ソリューション

❶「鉄は熱いうちに打て」は日本では通用しても海外ではとんでもない誤解
の原因となる。相手を批判したり、注意する場合、問題点をいきなりぶつ
ける対応は慎もう。

❷ フィードバックの項目を思い出そう。問題点は相手の良いところをほめた
後、どこを解決すればもっとよくなるかというスタンスで臨むべし。

❸ 全人格形成ではない。業務そのものの技量に集中した、具体的なアドバイ
スに徹するべし。

having the aspects of their work that are as yet immature or imperfect pointed out to them, the subordinates will gain the requisite skills and techniques as professionals while making all efforts to improve.

In Japan the conventional approach is that one has to "steal" the methods of one's superiors. People in junior positions gradually, over a long period of time, make the skills of their superiors their own, as they observe and copy their actions and approaches to work.

Many foreigners not only find it difficult to understand this Japanese way of going about things, but it can cause major misunderstandings, even having a negative effect on their relationship with the company.

Solution

❶ Although the idea of "striking while the iron is hot" is common in Japan, it can cause misunderstandings abroad. When criticizing or cautioning someone, refrain from abruptly hitting someone over the head with the problem.

❷ Remember the steps for giving feedback given above. The problem should be explained after complimenting the person, and you should take the approach of finding where you can make improvements to solve the problem.

❸ Give specific advice focusing not on the person's character, but rather on the skills necessary for that business.

事例

17

それは個人の領域。日本人はなんで首を
つっこんでくるんですか？

日本人の上司はときどき全く訳のわからない注意をする。僕の仕事とは
直接関係のない、全くどうでもいいようなことで。そしてそれにとても
こだわって、僕に押しつけてくるんだ。

外国人の不満　僕は日本の自動車会社のアメリカ支社で車のデザイン
を担当しています。自分で言うのもなんだけど、結構仕事はできるし、
技術者としてもしっかりした知識をもっていると思います。

　それなのに、ある日僕の日本人の上司が「君、**整理整頓**は仕事の基
本。ちゃんと机を片づけなさい」って注意したのです。ねえ、僕の仕
事の質と机の整理整頓とどんな**つながり**があるっていうのでしょう
か。僕の机のことは僕が決めます。そんなことまでとやかく言われ
たくありません。

　彼は僕の仕事の質は評価せずに、そんなプライベートなことに口
を出すのです。そもそも、彼は僕の仕事の出来不出来にはあまりは
っきりとした評価をしてくれません。むしろ、仕事とはまったく関
係のない、変なことで絡んでくるのです。理不尽ですよね。

　正直言ってこうした上司の対応には、うんざりしています。彼の
もとでこれからもちゃんとやっていけるかどうか、ちょっと不安で
す。やる気も失せちゃいますよ、まったく。

日本人の反論　我々の仕事は緻密な気配りと、精密なケアがあっては
じめて成り立つんです。だから、自分の机をちゃんと整頓できない
人に、どうしてしっかりとした仕事ができるっていうのでしょうか。

That's a private matter. Why do Japanese poke their noses into everything?

> Japanese superiors sometimes upbraid me for reasons I don't understand—about trivial things seemingly totally unrelated to work. Sometimes they go on and on and on, giving me quite a lecture.

Foreigner's grievance: I design cars for a Japanese automaker in America. I don't want to brag, but I'm good at my job. As a technician, I think I have a good grasp of what it takes.

But one day the guy I worked for just started to scold me, saying "Tidy up your desk. **Tidiness** is a basic part of your job." I mean, what **relevance** does the state of my desk have to whether I can do my job or not? It's up to me how I want to keep my desk. I don't have to be supervised by him in every little thing.

He doesn't place any value on what I actually do, but just pokes his nose into things that are none of his business. He's never given me any clear indication of whether he thinks I do my work well or not. Instead he picks fights with me about weird matters like my desk that are completely unrelated. It makes no sense.

Honestly, working with a guy like that as my superior makes me sick. I don't know if I can concentrate with him snooping around. It makes me want to just give up.

Japanese retort: The work in this company involves 100 percent care and attention to details. So if a person can't even tidy his desk, one has to wonder if he can do his job.

　彼はまだ若い。若い部下にそうした注意をするのは当然のことで
しょう。むしろ彼に育ってもらいたいから、そう言ったわけですが、
そんなふうにひねくれて解釈されているとは、正直言って失望して
います。彼なんか、まだこの業界で3年目でしょ。本当なら先輩の机
を拭いて、コピーをとって、その合間に基本的なことだけやってい
れば十分なんです。そうして少しずつ仕事を覚えていけば、本当の
プロへの道が開けるんですよ。

　だからね、机を整頓しろっていう**親心**をわかってほしいんです。
そんなことがどうして理解できないんでしょうか。

分析

　これは前事例で解説した、じっくりと時間をかけて部下を育て
ていこうというスタンスを持つ日本人と、ビジネスのスキルに基
づいたより直截なコミュニケーションを求める欧米人との意識面
での対立がもっとも顕著に現れたケースと言えましょう。

　フィードバックのノウハウを習得することに加えて、ぜひ知っ
ておいてほしいのが、注意する内容の取捨選択です。この場合、
もし整理整頓ができないがために、仕事に支障があるのであれば、
それを仕事の内容で注意し、机の問題はあくまでも個人の問題と
して、例えば、上司自らの経験談のような形で話すのであれば、
問題はないかもしれません。それなしに、部下に机の整頓を命令
しても逆効果です。

　自らの技能や仕事上の結果のみを基準として上司からの評価を
求める欧米の人には、仕事と直接関係のない机の整頓の話をされ
ても、ぴんとこないばかりか、プライベートな領域にずかずかと

He's a young fellow, so I tell him what I think—surely this is what I should do with someone so young—and I tell him because I want to help him improve. But if that's the twisted way he's going to interpret my good intentions, well, frankly, that's that. He's only been in this office for two years. Really, all that is required is for him to wipe down the desks of his superiors, make photocopies, and a few other basic things. It's by progressing gradually, learning what's involved in the job little by little, that he will find the road to becoming a true professional.

I wish he would understand and appreciate the **fatherly concern** I put into my requirement that he keep his desk tidy. Surely, it's obvious.

Analysis

This is one of the most glaring examples of the conflict in ways of thinking that exists between Japanese and Americans. As I explained in the previous case, the Japanese regard it as necessary to cultivate and educate junior colleagues thoroughly over a period of time, while Americans try for as direct communication as possible on the basis of business skills.

In addition to being familiar with how to give feedback, you should definitely know how to decide what to warn people about and what to leave alone. In this case, if the worker's inability to keep his desk clean becomes an obstacle to carrying out his work, you should warn him about it as it relates to job performance. The desk problem is an entirely personal one, so if, for example the superior was to talk about it based on his or her own experience, it would not be a problem. In other cases, ordering subordinates to clean their desks will have the opposite effect of what was intended.

Certainly, to most Americans and Westerners, who seek evaluation from their superiors on the basis only of job performance and results, when they are told to tidy up their desks, something that has

入ってこられたことに憤りすら覚えるかも知れません。

　しかし、こうしたアプローチの違いの背景には、上司があたか
も親のように若い部下の面倒を見ようとする日本流のメンタリテ
ィ以外に、もう一つの隠された文化上の違いがあるのです。**それは、
仕事において結果を重視する欧米の文化と、結果もさることなが
らプロセスにこだわる日本人との発想法との違いです。**

　仕事の結果がよければ、その手順や背景にある心の準備などは、
個々人が判断してやればよいと欧米の人は考えます。それに対し
て、日本人はともすれば、結果に至る心構えや仕事上の手順にこ
だわるのです。

　この違いは上司が部下に対して仕事の指導をするときに顕著に
現れます。シリコンバレーなどでは、高度な技術を駆使する仕事
をしていても、机の上は乱雑で、かつ方法論も独創的な人材は山
ほどいます。そうした独創性こそが、より良い仕事に繋がるとい
う意識すらあるのです。

　この場合、机を整理するということは、仕事の結果とは直接関
係ないだけでなく、よい結果を導くための無数にあるプロセスの
中の1つに過ぎないのです。

　そうした欧米流の発想で仕事をしている人が、日本流のプロセ
スを重視するアプローチに接した場合、そこからは単なる違い以
上の**軋轢が生まれて**しまいます。

　日本側は日本側で、欧米の人の仕事上の結果にもっと注目して、
冷静に評価するよう気を配りたいものです。

　また、欧米の人は日本人のそうした注意に対して、単に腹をた
てて反論するのではなく、その背景に悪意のないことを知って、
柔軟に対応しながら、日本文化を**よく知っている**第三者に仲介役

no direct bearing on their jobs, it will not only seem weird—they are likely to feel angry at having someone else **come trampling in** on their personal business.

But in the background is a particularly Japanese kind of mentality, whereby the superior tries to take charge of the needs of his junior colleagues. There is also another hidden cultural difference, which is in the way work is conceived of in the two cultures. Whereas **in the West the greatest importance is attached to results, in Japan people care about the process almost as much as the results.**

Westerners tend to think that as long as the results match up, judgments about the emotional preparation is up to the individual involved. By contrast, the Japanese care a great deal about the mental state during preparation leading up to the job just as much as the manner in which the job gets done.

This difference becomes most apparent in the way superiors direct the work of people under them. In workplaces in Silicon Valley, even when people are carrying out highly technically skilled work, the desks of these highly skilled, highly talented people may be in utter disarray—reflective of their completely idiosyncratic methodology. It's commonly thought that this is reflective of their originality, which is what leads them to produce the best work.

In such circumstances, whether their desks are tidy or not is irrelevant, and is only one of a large number of processes that can lead to good results.

When people who work under this kind of Western way of thinking come into contact with the Japanese approach, which attaches great importance to process, it **gives rise to friction** that goes beyond the mere difference itself.

The Japanese side should be advised to make their evaluations in an even-tempered way, paying more attention to the results in the workplace of the Westerners.

And I'd like Westerners to be aware that such directions from the Japanese are not meant in a spirit of contention—no malice exists behind the words. I suggest getting a third person, one who is **conversant with** Japanese culture, to act as a mediator, to explain and

になってもらって、欧米流の方法を日本人に理解してもらうよう
努めたいものです。

ソリューション

❶ 精神論では通用しない。精神論こそ日本の価値の押し付けになりかねない。日本の文化背景を持たない外国の人は、ただ戸惑い、あきれ、憤るだけ。

❷ フィードバックを行うときは、注意する内容の取捨選択に注意しよう。相手の技量や仕事上の結果のみを話題とするよう心がけよう。

❸ どうしても、個人の領域について話したいときは、1つの事例として自らの経験や体験談として話せば効果的。でも、けっして押し付けがましくならないよう、相手の意見も尊重しよう。

to help both sides understand the other.

Solution

❶ The Japanese spirit does not cross cultures, but Japanese values often end up getting pressed. For foreigners, who do not have a background in Japanese culture, it can be bewildering and tiresome, and cause resentment.

❷ When giving feedback, be careful about selecting which matters to bring to people's attention. Keep in mind that only things related to abilities and work results should be discussed.

❸ When you really want to talk about personal matters, it can be effective to give your personal experience or tell a story about something that happened to you as an example. Never be too pushy, though. Respect the other person's opinion.

僕も仲間に入れてよ。どうして日本人だけ でいつもかたまってしまうの？

日本人はどうしていつも日本人だけでかたまって、こそこそと話をして いるのでしょう。僕たちはいつものけ者。ガイジンってそんなに扱いに くい人種なの？

外国人の不満　僕はアメリカの日系企業に勤務しています。この会社、 アメリカ人は約300人で、日本人の駐在員が30人いるんだけど、彼 ら日本人はいつも一緒にこそこそとかたまって話をしている。ラン チのときもみんな連れだって外に出るし、夕方はまたみんな一緒に カラオケに行ったり、日系の飲み屋さんに行ったり。

　まあ、それくらいならいいんだけど、どうもそんな場所で、いろ んな重要な打ち合わせや合意が行われているようなんだ。僕たちは いつも**仲間外れ**。もちろん夜まで彼らのカラオケにつき合う気はな いけどね。

　そもそも、そんなとこでこっそりと物事を決めたり、暗黙の了解 をしたりすることがフェアな行為とは思えないですよね。僕たちは この国ではちゃんとキャリアも積んだプロなんですよ。ビジネスな んだから、なんでオフィスで我々を交えて意思決定をしないのでしょ う。僕たちには結局「ああしろこうしろ」って、決まった方針しか 伝えてこないんだから。**げんなりですよ**。

日本人の反論　考えてもみてください。僕たちは、いつも慣れない外 国で、英語を使って苦労してるんですよ。ランチの時ぐらい、たま

Let me into your group. Why do Japanese always stick together only with other Japanese?

Why is it that Japanese people always huddle in groups with other Japanese, and conduct secret discussions? We're always excluded. Are foreigners so difficult for them to deal with?

Foreigner's grievance: I'm working for a Japanese corporation that has a branch in the United States. The branch here consists of about three hundred Americans and thirty Japanese workers. These Japanese always go about in groups, being secretive. Even during lunch breaks, they all go out together, keeping to themselves. Then when evening comes they go out together again, whether to karaoke bars or Japanese drinking joints.

Well, if it was just a matter of socializing, I could understand. But no, apparently they have all sorts of important discussions and come to secret agreements in such places. We Americans are always **left out**. Not that we want to go with them, even after work, to karaoke bars.

This kind of behavior—deciding things in secret, coming to exclusive understandings with each other—is just not honest, in my opinion. We're fully qualified professionals, you know—we have solid careers behind us. Why can't they include us in their decisions about work at the office? In the end, we just get given orders to do this or that when decisions have already been made. **It really ticks us off**.

Japanese retort: Think for a moment. We're working so hard in a foreign country, using English all the time. It's natural, at least during lunch break, that we want to take a rest, speak Japanese and

には息抜きをして、日本の話をしたいし、本社のうわさ話なんかも聞きたいでしょ。アメリカ人だって、よく見ると人種や出身国の人たちだけでかたまったりしてるじゃないですか。同じことだと思うんですよ。

それにね、アメリカのオフィスより何倍も大きくて複雑に組織の入り組んだ本社のことを知っているのは我々なんだから、彼らのために本社とのコンセンサスをとろうとしている努力もわかってほしい。そのために日本人同士で意見交換したりすることも必要なんですよ。

我々はね、本社や日本の事情を何にも知らない現地の人からの強い要望や、プレゼンテーションを受けて、それを日本側と**すり合わせ**、お互いにうまくいくように骨を折らなければならないんです。いわばサンドウィッチになっているわけで、そんな我々が集まってああでもないこうでもないって意見交換をしてどこが悪いんですか。

しかも、彼らアメリカ人は、自分のプロとしてのキャリアばかり強調して、日本のことを勉強しようとか、理解しようとかいう意識がないんです。入社するときは日本語も勉強したいなんて調子のいいことを言って、その意志を完遂する人なんて1人もいないんです。だから、我々だって、そんな彼らと日本との間に立って悩まざるを得ないのです。少しくらいわかってくださいよ。

exchange gossip about things that are going on at the company in Japan. And actually, I see quite a few Americans who stick in the same groups—people of the same ethnicity, or who've come from the same country. Why shouldn't we do the same?

Plus, we'd like them to appreciate what a task it is to get a consensus with the guys over at the main office in Japan on their behalf, since *we* are the ones who are familiar with all the intricate goings-on at the head office in Japan, which is so much larger than the branch in the States. This is one reason why we have to exchange opinions amongst ourselves in Japanese.

When the people here, who don't know a thing about conditions in Japan, present us with their proposals for projects with Japan, making a strong case for them, we have to go to a lot of trouble to get them to **fit with** the Japanese way, and get headquarters to see our point of view so that both sides can approve. We're "sandwiched," if you like, between the two sides. What's wrong with our meeting to have a detailed exchange of opinions?

Also, all those guys do is push their own careers—they show no interest in trying to find out about or appreciate Japan. When they first join up they say all sorts of enthusiastic things about learning the Japanese language and so on—but no one actually follows through on this. So, naturally, in our position stuck in the middle, we can't help but get irritated sometimes. Why can't they show a little more understanding?

分析

　日本の企業は、世界で仕事をしていく上で大きな構造的な問題を抱えています。それは、意思決定がいつも組織の中枢で行われていて、現地組織に**権限を委譲**できずにいることです。

　したがって、駐在員は現地での重要な案件が浮上してくると、本社とのすり合わせや、本社とつながりの深い駐在員同士でのコンセンサスの構築に時間を費やすことになります。

　問題は、現地で採用された人が、こうした**輪の外に置かれ**がちであるということです。現地への権限委譲は、日系企業が世界に根を下ろしていく上で、乗り越えていかなければならない大きなハードルなのです。

　一方、日系企業に働く外国人も理解しなければならないことがあります。それは、日系企業はいわゆる西欧社会という全く異なった文化背景を持つ環境の中で、いかに人のモチベーションを向上させ、生産性を上げていくかというテーマに日々悩んでいるという事実です。その悩みはビジネス文化が違うだけに深刻で、時には彼らの善意が現地の人には悪意にとられたりというジレンマを経験しているのです。

　柔軟性を持って、日本人との人間関係を構築し、日本について学ぶ姿勢を持ちながら、日本側に現地の常識やニーズを伝えていくという、いわば日常業務の中には存在しない、もう1つのタスクが自分にあることを欧米の人も理解し、積極的に対応するべきなのです。

　文化背景の違う人が1つの組織に集まって働く場合、そうした目

Analysis

There is one great structural disadvantage in Japanese corporations that always makes for tremendous difficulty when they take their industries abroad. This is that the decision-making is always carried out at the very nucleus, the main office, which seems unwilling or unable to **delegate authority** to the overseas branch.

Accordingly, when something important arises overseas, the Japanese working there have to spend a lot of time getting everybody in the main office in Japan to agree as well as getting a consensus with Japanese working in other companies who also have a close relationship with the main office in Japan.

The problem is that the local workers in those countries abroad tend to **get left out of the loop**. Delegating authority to branch companies overseas is one hurdle that it is vital to cross if Japanese corporations really want their businesses to grow sturdily around the world.

On the other hand, non-Japanese who work for Japanese companies need to understand something. That is that Japanese corporations are greatly concerned about how to raise productivity and stimulate motivation in their workers in this foreign environment, which has a completely different cultural background from the one they are used to. Their worry grows the more markedly business culture in those countries differs from their own. Sometimes their good intentions can be taken as having questionable motivations by the people of the country concerned.

Develop a flexible attitude, build up relationships with Japanese people, and adopt a position of wanting to learn about Japan—and also, while you are doing this, let the Japanese side know what you consider common sense and what you need—this should be part of your daily routine. Foreign nationals working for these companies should realize that it is up to them to express their needs, and they should approach the problem in a "can-do" way.

When people of different cultures work in the same place for the

に見えないタスクは、必要不可欠な業務の一つなのです。その結果、柔軟に判断し対応するノウハウが育まれ、組織も個人もグローバルなレベルに成長していくのです。もちろん、これは日本人駐在員にも強調したいことなのですが……。

ソリューション

❶ 商談や議論には海外の人も積極的に仲間に入れよう。どんなに異文化の管理が難しくても、仲間はずれでは何も進まない。

❷ 権限を現地にいかに委譲していくか。これは海外で活動する日系企業の大きな悩み。しかし、このハードルを越えなければ、本当の成長は見込めない。

❸ 本社の代表者ではない。現地の人と現地のために本社と話しているんだというスタンスをもてるよう、心がけよう。

same organization, these kinds of tasks, which are not immediately obvious, are, in fact, a vital part of one's work. If they are carried out properly, people build up the knowhow to make judgments flexibly, and both the organization and the individuals evolve into global-level participants. I want to stress this particularly for those Japanese who are working for Japanese companies abroad.

Solution

❶ Actively try to include foreigners in negotiations or discussions. No matter how difficult it is to manage cultural differences, nothing will be accomplished if people get left out.

❷ How much authority to transfer to the local office is a big worry for Japanese companies operating abroad. However, if you do not clear this hurdle, do not expect any growth.

❸ Keep in mind that you are not representatives of headquarters. Take the attitude that you are speaking on behalf of the local office with them.

日本人はなんであんな人を採用しようとするのだろうか？

日本人は、我々から見てまったく理解できないような人材を採用する。そして、仕事ができないのに、ただ仲良くやれるおとなしい人材だけが評価される。いったいどうなっているのでしょうか？

外国人の不満　ロンドンから日本に駐在してきて今日本での生産性の向上に取り組んでいます。そのために、コスト感覚があって業務管理のできる優秀な人材を採用しようと思っているのですが、それがなかなかうまくいきません。

　我々は常に仕事の効率と、そのための有能な人材の投入を考えています。この厳しい競争を勝ち抜くには当然のことでしょう。ちゃんと自らをアピールでき、強い主張をもったプロの人材を獲得したいと思うのです。

　ところが日本人は違うんです。こいつは**チームプレイ**ができないだろうとか、自己主張が強すぎる人間は信用できないとか、ときにはどうも性格に問題がありそうだなどと言って我々がこれはと思う人をことごとく却下するんです。

　ビジネスの場は戦場です。チームプレイも大切ですが、即座に戦える強い個性をもった人材のほうがどれだけ役に立つことか。彼らがいったい何を**基準**に人を選んでいるのか、わからなくなります。

Why do the Japanese hire that kind of person?

> The Japanese employ people to work for them for reasons that are incomprehensible in our eyes. The quiet people, the ones who don't assert themselves at all, are the ones who get the best evaluations—even though they are not necessarily good at their jobs. What's going on?

Foreigner's grievance: I moved from London to Japan and am now working on ways of improving production. In order to do that, I wanted to hire some capable, cost-conscious staff with management skills, but so far it hasn't gone well.

We make it a habit always to put efficiency first, and we like to employ talented, capable people, people who will contribute to our efficiency. Surely this goes without saying—it's the only way to get ahead in all this ferocious competition. We want to get people who are professional, who can assert themselves, and who can show what they are made of.

But Japanese have different priorities. They reject anyone we consider worth employing, almost without exception—and for reasons like: oh, this person doesn't look as if he'll **toe the line**; or, that person has too strong an ego; he or she can't be trusted—and sometimes just on the grounds that a person looks like they might have a personality problem.

It's a battle zone out there in the business world. Sure, it's important to get along with people—but how much more useful are people who have a strong sense of self, who can put up a strong fight for what they want. I just don't understand the **criteria** Japanese use for hiring people.

日本人の反論 よく外国人が採用する人間は、採用される前にはあれもできるこれもできると結構威勢がいいんですが、いざ仕事をさせてみるとそれほどうまくいかない人が多いんです。自己PRばかりで同僚のことを考えない利己的な人材がたくさんいます。

我々は会社という組織を運営し、その組織力で競争に打ち勝っていかなければならないわけで、身勝手な行動をしたり、よそを向いていたりしては効率よく業務ができません。

一匹狼よりも、気配りができ、ねばり強く仕事に取り組める人材が必要なんです。外国の人はどうしてそこのところが理解できないんでしょうか。彼らの言う通りに人を採用していったら、組織がばらばらになってしまいます。

分析

日本人が美徳とする価値観と欧米の人がよしとする価値観には大きな違いがあります。当然、人を評価するとき、そうした価値観が**評価基準**に大きな影響を与えるわけですから、日本人と外国人とではそこにずれが生まれてしまうのは当然なのです。

外国人が日本で仕事をするときに、英語ができる日本人、あるいはプレゼンテーションがうまくて**雄弁な**日本人を過大評価して採用したりすることがよくあります。逆に日本人は、日本人の言うことをよくきく馴染みやすいアメリカ人を評価する傾向にあるようです。そして、結局はどちらもうまくいかなかったということも間々あります。

例えば、先に述べたように、面接にきた人が「なんでもさせていただきます」と言えば、日本人の担当者は控えめながらもやる気の

Japanese retort: So often the applicants foreigners want to employ make all sorts of boasts before they're employed that they can do this or that—and then when you actually try to get them to do those things, you find that they can't. A lot of people just put themselves first, selling themselves, and don't care about their coworkers at all.

We are running a company, an organization—we have to survive and get ahead on the strength of our power as an organization. If one person starts acting entirely for him- or herself, or thinking about personal goals, efficiency goes down.

Rather than lone wolves, we'd prefer to employ people who can be considerate and cooperative, and who don't give up easily. I can't understand why this is so incomprehensible to foreigners. If we employed the people they say we should, the company would fall apart.

Analysis

Japanese and Westerners employ a totally different set of values to determine "good" and "bad" in their assessments of situations. Naturally, these values have an influence on the **yardsticks** by which people are evaluated—and thus differences of opinion are bound to arise between foreigners and Japanese.

Often when foreigners work in Japan they employ Japanese people, over-estimating their ability because they can speak English well or are very **eloquent** when they make presentations. And conversely, Japanese tend to value Americans more who listen to what they say, and who they find more comfortable to be with. And frequently, in both cases, things do not turn out as well as expected.

In the case above, for example, when someone comes for an interview and says, "I am willing to do any kind of work," a Japanese would probably think this person is rather retiring, but shows energy and is

あるエネルギッシュな人材だと思うかもしれません。しかし、アメリカ人は同じ人に対して、個性のない、自らをアピールできない退屈な人材だと思ってしまいます。価値観が違えば、1つのメッセージも両極端に捉えられてしまうのです。その国ではどのような人が優秀かということをお互いによく理解する必要があるのは、そうした理由によるのです。

国際企業では、それぞれの国の中でうまく活動でき、違う文化にも自らを適応させることのできる人材が強く求められています。そのためにも、会社のミッションを理解した上で、人材を正しく採用し評価できる現地の社員をしっかりと育て、その人に権限を与えることが大切です。

ソリューション

❶ 人の善し悪しを判断する基準はそれぞれの国の文化によって、異なっている。日本人がよしとする人を海外の人は必ずしも評価しないことを知っておこう。

❷ 日本人の言うことをきく外国人に惑わされる日本人。英語がうまくプレゼンがうまい日本人に惑わされる欧米人。これはクラシックなケースなのだ。

❸ 双方の文化背景を理解して、ブリッジとなれる人材こそ、国際企業が求める貴重な人材だ。

keen on the job. An American, on the other hand, would assume that the person lacks personality, that he or she is an uninteresting person who is unable to show him- or herself off in a good light. The same message can be taken in two totally different ways, depending on one's value system. This is why it is necessary for both parties to fully understand what kind of person is considered to be of value in the other country.

The kind of people who are required for international corporations are those who can do their jobs no matter what country they are in—who can adapt easily to a different culture. This is one of the reasons why you should try to foster connections in the countries where you have branch companies who can hire the right kind of people for the job, knowing what the company wants of them, and what the company's mission is—and give such people authority.

Solution

❶ How people's strengths and weaknesses are evaluated varies depending on the culture of a country. Be aware that people that are seen as good workers in Japan may not be evaluated the same way by foreigners.

❷ Japanese are taken in by foreigners who listen to what they say. Foreigners are taken in by Japanese who speak English well or are eloquent when giving presentations. These are classic mistakes.

❸ International companies want talented, valuable people who can understand differing cultural backgrounds and bridge gaps.

チームワークとグループ活動を混同する日本人

日本人は、いつまでたっても独立して歩こうとしない。何かプロジェクトがあって、それが終了しても、やれアフターケアだ、やれ次の指示が欲しいと言って過去のチームから巣立っていかないのはどうしてなんだ!?

外国人の不満　私は、通信関連のグローバル企業で働くイラン人の技術者です。もっとも、母国を離れたのは子供のころで、今の国籍はアメリカですが。仕事柄いろいろな国の人とチームを組んで、新しいプロジェクトを推進します。

　そんな中、時々日本人がいつまでも親鳥から離れられない甘えん坊の小鳥みたいに見えることがあるのです。彼らは、プロジェクトが終了しても、いつまでも我々の指示や支援を求めて離れようとしない。我々は常に未来に向かって新しいことに取り組まなければなりません。それだけに、もう過ぎてしまった過去にいつまでも停滞して**面倒を見て**ほしいという日本側の要求には応えられないんです。

　もし、日本人がアフターサービスを求めるのならば、我々には立派な得意先からの要求や苦情に応じるカスタマーサービス部門があるから、そこに問い合わせればいいじゃないですか。いちいち我々の後を追いかけてくる必要はないのです。そうした部門とネットワークして、自分の力で解決するように努めてほしいんですよ。

　自立できないかぎり、その組織は成長しません。そうした意味で、我々は日本側の能力に疑問をもちはじめています。

日本人の反論　欧米の人は無責任ですよ。自分たちの仕事が終わればさっさと**引き上げて**、別のプロジェクトに移動してしまう。我々と

The Japanese confuse "teamwork" with "group activities"

Japanese don't seem to be able to act independently. Whenever we work on a project with them and the project is over, they ask for "after-care," or instructions as to what to do next. They just don't seem to be able to leave the nest of whatever team they've been working with!

Foreigner's grievance: I'm an engineer from Iran and work for a global communications company. I left my home country when I was a child, and am now an American citizen. In this line of work, we often form teams with people from various countries to move forward on new projects.

In those situations, the Japanese seem to be like fledgling birds who never leave the safety and comfort of their parents' nest. Even after a project is over, they keep asking for our instructions or support. We want to get on, get ahead, and get involved in new projects—move forward into the future. The work we did with them is past—we can't be doing this with requests that we stay where we are and continue to **look after** their needs when the job is over and done with.

If the Japanese do need some special attention after a sale, a department exists that deals precisely with that kind of thing: the Customer Service Department, which handles claims and complaints from our clients. Why don't they take their inquiries there? There's no need to hang on to us for every little thing—I wish they would make the effort to connect with that department and solve the problem on their own.

No organization will grow if it's that dependent. It makes us wonder whether the Japanese know what they're doing.

Japanese retort: Well, we think Westerners are just irresponsible. As soon as whatever they're doing is done, **off they go**, on a new

一緒に仕事をしたことなんてなかったかのように去っていって、あとのことには知らん顔なんです。

一度は同じ釜の飯を食ったわけでしょ。それなら、我々が得意先からクレームを受けているとき、もう知らないよと言うのではなく、せめてアメリカサイドでコーディネートして、協力してくれないと困るんです。だって、カスタマーサービス部門に問い合わせても、彼らは過去の経緯はなにも知らないから、同じ説明を何度もしなければならない。だいいち彼らは日本の得意先がいかに**うるさい**かなんてことは全く理解していませんからね。

そもそも、どうして彼らは仕事を異動するときにちゃんと引き継ぎをして、我々がその後戸惑わないように配慮しないんでしょう。人が変わればすべて**一から**やりなおし。しかも、そのために使う労力と手間は大変です。もっと、しっかりと責任感をもって業務に携わってもらいたいものです。

分析

外資系に勤務したことのある日本人なら、少なからずこうした悩みを持っているのではないでしょうか。ここに見られる日本人と欧米人、特にアメリカ人との意識の違いは、それこそ、未来志向のビジネス文化と過去とのつながりを重んじるビジネス文化とが生みだした摩擦なのです。これについては、次の項でもさらに詳しく解説します。

アメリカ人は、プロジェクトを推進するにあたって、それをチームワークによって進めていきます。すなわち、チームとはそのプロジェクトのために集まってきて、そのプロジェクトが終われば解散し、次の業務へと拡散していくことを前提としているので

project. They take off just as if the project we have been involved in together never existed—they don't seem to care at all about what happens afterwards.

But surely, once you have worked with another person, it's as if you've eaten from the same dish. That's what we think, so when we get complaints from our clients, we never say, "Well, that's nothing to do with us"—we try at least to coordinate with the overseas side and see what we can do. If we tried to take the complaint to the Customer Service Department, who don't have any knowledge of the history of the project, we'd have to go to the trouble of explaining the whole story over again. Furthermore, they have no idea just how **fussy** our Japanese clients are.

And why, when they do move on to the next project, can't they show some consideration and keep up a connection with us—so that we don't find ourselves in difficulties? A change of personnel means that everything has to be done again **from scratch**. Think of the effort and time involved. I wish they would conduct themselves in our group projects with a more proper sense of responsibility.

Analysis

Any Japanese who has worked for a foreign capital venture will have been bothered to some extent by the kind of issue we see occurring here. The difference in thinking we see between Japanese and Westerners, particularly Americans, is the friction between a business culture that faces the future and a culture where great significance is given to relationships in the past. This is something I will go into more deeply in the next case.

When Americans get on with a project, they go about it with "teamwork." And a premise of the term is the idea that the people who come together for that particular project disperse when it is over, and go their separate ways on to the next job. By contrast, Japanese look for "group" activity which continues from the past into the present,

す。それに対して、日本人は過去から現在、そして未来へと継続したグループ活動を求めてきます。そんな日本人から見ると、解散して次の未来へと去っていくアメリカ人が無責任に見えるのです。しかも日本の得意先も**過去から未来へ**と一貫したサービスを求めますから、この摩擦は深刻です。

　アメリカ人は、チームを解散するにあたって、例えばアフターサービスなどに関連した案件を、別の部門に託していきます。その部門では、情報をマニュアル化することによって、対応するシステムになっています。日本人から見ると、全く過去を理解していない別の部門が、マニュアルだけで対応してくるわけですから不安がつのります。**かゆいところに手が届かない**アメリカ側の対応に苛立つのです。

　こうした摩擦を解決するには、プロジェクトが完成し、チームが解散するにあたって、日本人とアメリカ人との適切な人的交流の場を設けて、両者が未来へ向けてのコーディネートをするように努めるのが一番でしょう。

　日本の中に日本のことが理解できるアメリカ人が、そしてアメリカの中に、アメリカのそうした**未来志向**を理解しながらうまく日本との間をつなぐことのできる日本人がいて、お互いに連携していけばいいのです。そのためにも、時間をかけてそうした人材を育てるよう、日頃から努力したいものです。

ソリューション

❶ グループではない、チームなのだ。チームはプロジェクトが終われば解消し、みんな未来に羽ばたく。この異文化を理解しておこう。

❷ 日本と同じように、いつまでも同じ人がケアすることを期待するな。もちろん、引き継ぎだってしっかりとニーズを言わない限り、充分には行われない。

❸ 日本のアフターケアについて、そのニーズと経済効果をしっかりと相手に伝えよう。黙っていてもアフターケアがあると期待するなかれ。

and then on into the future. From the point of view of these Japanese, the way Americans disperse and go on to whatever is happening next seems irresponsible. Moreover, Japanese clients expect the kind of service that endures **from the past on into the future**—so the resulting friction is no small matter.

Once a team that has worked on a project has dispersed, Americans tend to pass issues relating to customer service and complaints on to a completely separate department. This department has a system where it deals with matters by the book. From the Japanese point of view, this is a worrying situation—a completely different case with no knowledge of the lead-up to a certain situation deals with their problems using just a manual. The Japanese feel irritation with what they see as a **lackadaisical** quality on the American part.

In order to deal with this sort of friction, when a project is over and the team dissolves, the best thing is to set up a place for both sides to have some sort of interchange so that they can still have the opportunity to coordinate in the future.

It would be good if Americans in Japan with a good understanding of Japanese ways could hook up with Japanese who understand the **forward-looking spirit** of America and who coordinate with the Japan side so that both can work together. This is another reason why it is good to put regular effort and time into developing people who are capable of doing this.

Solution

❶ It is not a group—it is a team. If the team finishes a project, it is dissolved. Everyone should spread their wings and move forward to the future. Understand this cultural difference.

❷ Do not expect that the same person will take care of you forever like happens in Japan. Of course, if you do not express your needs when taking over a job, you probably won't get enough support.

❸ Tell your partner about Japanese "after-care", the needs associated with it, and its economic benefits. Do not expect "after-care" if you do not ask for it.

過去は過去。未来志向でいこうよ、日本人!

> 日本人は合理的じゃないですね。だって、別の会社や個人のほうが明らかに仕事ができるのに、その会社をよく知っているとか、その人とのつきあいが長いというだけで、新しい参入者を許さないんですから。

外国人の不満　私はドイツに本社のある、世界へネットワークをもつ医療品企業で、シンガポールから1年前に日本の支社に支社長として赴任しました。最近の不況で、なんとか会社の実績を上げようと、いろいろと努力しているのですが、日本人の部下がなかなかそれを受け入れてくれません。

　というのも、本社から推薦されて、私はいつも会社に新しい業者を紹介しようとするんですが、日本人はなかなかそれを認めようとしないんです。こちらのほうが利益率もよくて、迅速に対応できるにもかかわらず、**昔からのつき合いにこだわって新しい参入者を**なかなか受け入れようとはしません。

　日本の会社は決裁をするのに時間がかかる構造になっていることは知っています。でも、それだけではない、新しいものを排除しようという極めて排他的な考え方が日本の企業の中にあるように思えます。

　人の採用だってそうじゃないですか。どんなに優秀な人材がいても、日本人はいまだに学歴にこだわったりする。時には、実力はそっちのけにして、性格や過去の人間関係などを重視する。合理的とは思えません。しかも、昔この会社はこうだったなどと理屈をつけて、

The past is the past. Look to the future, Japanese people.

> The Japanese just aren't rational. I mean, often even when they know quite well that a different company or another individual would be better for a job, they don't allow them to participate, saying simply that they know such-and-such a company better, or that their association with such-and-such a person is longstanding.

Foreigner's grievance: I work for a medical supplies company headquartered in Germany, which has a global network of offices. I was transferred from Singapore to work as the branch manager of the Japanese office one year ago. Because of the recent recession, I want to improve the company's performance somehow, and have been making various efforts to do so, but my Japanese staff never seems to accept it.

That is to say, I'm always trying to introduce new businesses to the company at the recommendation of headquarters, but the Japanese just will not accept them. Even though the people I introduce have better profit ratings, and can deal with matters promptly, the Japanese care more about **longstanding associations** and refuse even to try anyone new.

I realize Japanese companies are set up in a way that necessitates a certain amount of time in the decision-making process. But it's not just that: it seems to me that an extremely exclusive way of thinking prevails in Japanese companies that tries to exclude anything new.

Look at when they employ people for jobs: no matter how capable a person may be, the Japanese still pay much more attention to his academic record—whether he or she has gone to university, etc. Sometimes, they attach so much importance to character and a person's past connections, and completely disregard a person's actual

現在の実力やスタンスを見ようという気持ちがありません。

　ビジネスの場ではもっと割り切って、生産性の向上という大前提からいろんな決裁をしなければならないと思うんですが。私は、そんな日本人のポリシーに挑戦することをすでに諦めかけているんですよ。

日本人の反論　人間関係ってそんなに単純なものじゃないし、簡単に構築されるものじゃないでしょう。それなのに、彼らは目先の利害だけにとらわれて、長期的な視野もなく物事を決めようとするんです。そしていつも、**何でそんなに合理的じゃないんだって**我々に食ってかかる。我々の深い配慮や、長年培ってきた人間関係に基づく仕事の進め方を全く理解しようとしないんです。

　彼らはそれがたとえ新しい参入者であってもマニュアルがしっかりしてさえいれば、ちゃんと仕事を伝達できると思っている。そんなもんじゃないでしょ。ビジネスは常に緊急事態の連続です。そんなときにはマニュアルなんて役には立たない。こうしてほしいって言えば、あうんの呼吸で相手にその要望が伝わる信頼関係が培われていなければ、物事はうまく運ばないじゃないですか。

　過去に起きたことを斟酌することなく、未来に進むことは不可能ですよね。でも彼らは、それはもう過去のこと。だから忘れてこれからのことを考えようって言うのです。だから同じ間違いを繰り返してしまうのです。

　それに、彼らが言うほど決裁は簡単じゃない。十分に他の関係者とのコンセンサスを取ってリスクをつぶして前に進むという、ビジネスの基本がわかっていないのです。

ability—it isn't rational. Furthermore, they add all sorts of illogical reasons, for example citing the reputation a company used to have in the past, not interested at all in whether it is actually any good at the present time.

It's my belief that in business, decisions should be made with the main requisite being to achieve an increase in productivity. Already I feel like, "Why should I bother even to try when this is the policy of the Japanese company?"

Japanese retort: Human relationships are complicated; it takes time to build them up. Nevertheless, the only thing those Americans seem to worry about is the immediate benefit—they decide everything from a short-term point of view, and then they come and accuse us, telling us we're so **irrational**. They make no attempt to understand the deep consideration we give to what we do, and the way we do our work based on relationships that we have fostered over many years.

They think that even if we bring in some new person or company to do the job, as long as we make an effective manual to teach them, the new person will master the work adequately. But surely it's not that simple. Business always involves reacting to the unexpected—swift action and on-the-spot decisions. Manuals and suchlike will be of no use in these situations. Unless relations of trust have been built up so that you know when you say, "I want you to do this," there will be unspoken communication and he or she will do exactly what you want, things are bound to go wrong.

Progress is impossible without trying to learn some lessons from the past. But for them, well, that's over, it's in the past, so let's forget it and just get on with the next thing, is what they say. And this is why the same mistakes keep getting repeated.

Also, making a decision isn't as easy as they say it is. They don't understand the basics of business in Japan—getting an adequate consensus with all the other people involved, and trying as much as possible to eliminate all the risks.

彼らは、いとも簡単に人と契約して、仕事が終われば赤の他人になってしまう。それじゃあ会社にノウハウが蓄積するはずがないでしょう。

もっとも彼らは次から次へと職場を変えるし、職場自体も他社とくっついたり離れたりと動きが激しいので、じっくりと腰を据えてビジネスに**取り組め**ないんでしょうか。今、早急に実績を上げて自分の手柄にして昇進したいってことばかり考えているから、こうした短兵急な手当をしようとするのかもしれません。

分析

世界各国のビジネス文化には、過去をいち早く清算して未来へ向かおうとする文化と、過去と未来とが**渾然一体**となって先に進もうという文化があります。日本のように、千年以上に渡って脈々と文化を育ててきた国の人は、往々にして過去をしっかりと振り返りながら前に進もうとします。

それに対して、多様な文化背景の人が一つ所に集まって新たな文化を創ろうとする国では、過去のことを語り合う前にまず未来への道順をつけようとします。このプロセスの違いが摩擦を生むのです。

過去の人間関係に基づいた一貫性のあるビジネス関係をよしとする日本人と、あたかも移民同士が集まって社会をつくってきた背景をそのままビジネスに持ち込んで、合理的であれば過去にこだわらずダイナミックに物事を変化させ、ビジネス上の人間関係も変えていこうとする人々との意識の隔たりは思った以上に大きいのです。

This is why they make contracts with people so easily, and then when the job is over become strangers again. What knowhow is going to be accumulated if this is how a company works?

Of course, they go from one job to another without a second thought, leaving and joining firms—and the companies themselves are always merging with and then separating from other corporations—so maybe they just can't **get to grips with** business in a thoroughgoing way. The only thing they think about is making their resumes look as impressive as possible so that they can get ahead—that's why they take such risks.

Analysis

Business cultures of countries around the world can be divided into two basic types: the type that always wants to move on from the past forward into the future, and the type that moves forward with the idea that the past and the future exist in a **continuum**. People from countries like Japan, which has had its own culture for over a thousand years, move into the future cautiously, always looking over their shoulder into the past.

By contrast, in America, for example, where people with diverse cultural backgrounds have gathered together and are trying to create a new culture, rather than think about the past, they want above all else to construct a modus operandum for the future. This difference in methodology gives rise to friction.

The gap in thinking between the Japanese, who tend to value consistent business relations using relationships that have been formed over the course of many years, and Americans, whose society is, after all, composed of many groups of immigrants who wanted to build a new society and who bring this cultural background into the workplace—not clinging to the ways of the past and instead enjoying change, even *trying* to bring about changes—is much larger than one would suppose.

　今世界で活動している欧米のグローバル企業の多くが、日本型とはまったく違う後者のビジネス文化をもって活動しています。

　日本人から見ると、未来志向のやり方には**不安がつきまとい**ます。まず前に進めてみて、リスクが生まれればその場所で考えながら対処しようとするそうした**決裁方法**は、過去を踏まえながら、コンセンサスを培って、じっくりと時間をかけて決裁し、リスクを潰した後に前に進もうとする日本人にはなかなか馴染めないのです。

　したがって、ここでは双方の歩み寄りがどうしても必要になります。欧米人は過去の資料や実績を慎重に吟味し、どのように前に進めばいいのかを日本人と心を開いて打ち合わせるスタンスが必要です。

　そして、日本人には、現実のニーズをしっかりと認識した上で、より迅速に決裁し、未来志向で物事を考えていく柔軟性が問われています。

　ただ、日本側も昔の経験に固執せず、ドアを閉めずに、まず彼らの要望を根付かせるためにどうするか、ソリューションを検討する姿勢を持つことは大切です。何が困難かという点から、それを克服するにはどうすればよいかという点まで、心を開いて欧米人と情報を交換するスタンスをもちましょう。

　そして、本社の意向に耳を傾けながらも、現場の意思と**調整**し、双方とも現場にできるだけ決裁権を委譲しながら、ビジネスを進めてゆく環境を整えることです。大きな企業であればあるほど、このような構造改革を双方が共同で進めていくべきなのです。

Most of the Western companies which are active around the world today are different from Japanese companies, which have the latter form of business culture.

From the Japanese point of view, a way of doing things which puts emphasis on the future is **bound to be insecure**. Firstly, Japanese have great difficulty with that style of **decision-making method**, which involves making the decision to go ahead and dealing with risks when and as they arise. The Japanese like to move forward with projects only having spent a long time mulling over various situations that occurred in the past, having tried to pare down the possibility of risk to a minimum, and then finally come to a consensus.

Since this is the case, the first requirement is to find some way of bringing both sides nearer to each other in their ways of thinking. The Western side should take a stance of trying to assess carefully and sincerely data and achievements from the past, and having meetings with the Japanese side in a frank, open-hearted way about what steps to take to move forward with the work.

And the Japanese have to become more flexible: after getting a thorough grasp of the actual requirements of a situation, they should try to come to a quicker decision, and think about matters with a more forward-looking attitude.

However, it is important for the Japanese side to first actively consider solutions for fulfilling their requests without relying too much on past experience or shutting doors. Adopt a stance in which you exchange information with Westerners with an open mind to not only find out what the difficulty is but what should be done to overcome it.

It is important to create an environment where it is possible to carry out business while listening to what headquarters wants, and **conciliating** it with what the people on site want, delegating things to the people on site as much as possible. The larger a corporation is, the more necessary it is for both sides to cooperate with each other in making this kind of systemic change.

ソリューション

❶ 過去にこだわりながらそこから未来をみるのではなく、未来に向けて歩き出しながら調整するビジネスの進め方を理解しよう。

❷ 日本の顧客が過去の事例を大切にしていることを、欧米のパートナーにはしっかりと説明しよう。

❸ 過去にとらわれず、未来志向の海外からの提案に積極的に心を開こう。それを日本の風土になじませていくことこそ、国際企業での駐在員の役割なのだから。

Solution

❶ Keep in mind that rather than viewing the future while fixating on the past, you have to understand how to do business by making adjustments while moving forward.

❷ Explain to your Western partners clearly how much importance Japanese customers place on past example.

❸ Rather than fixating on the past, try actively to be open-minded when you receive future-oriented proposals from abroad. The role of exparts in international companies is to adapt them to the cultural climate of Japan.

事例

22

責任領域がはっきりしない日本企業では、自分を伸ばせないよ!!

> 日本人は本当に自分のキャリアのことを考えているんでしょうか。もっと自分のキャリアと直結した業務を責任をもってこなしたほうがいいのではと思うのですが。彼らは単なる会社人間で、専門家ではないんです。

外国人の不満　私はイギリスで日系の企業に勤めていたのですが、最近日本の本社に2年間の予定で出向してきています。

しかし、こちらにきて、少々がっかりしていることがあるんです。というのも、日本人の上司は、私のキャリアのことをほとんど考えてくれないんです。私がプロとして、どのように専門的な知識やスキルを身につけていきたいかといった希望に彼らは耳を傾けてくれません。そして、いつも会社のニーズを優先し、我々に我慢を強いるんです。よく見ていると、同僚の日本人も自分のキャリアよりも会社のニーズを優先しています。ある人なんか、会社の要望で**配置転換**され、営業部門から人事部門へと異動したりしています。でも、彼らは我々ほど不満そうではない。いったいなぜなんでしょうか?

私は、自分のキャリアのために会社で働き、そのためには明解な責任領域のある仕事をやりたいのです。あいまいではなく、これこそが私のやらなければならない業務だというような仕事が。そうすれば、他の人との業務の分担もはっきりとして、仕事自体もやりやすくなるはずですよね。

そう考えた時、日本の組織は、責任領域自体があいまいで従業員はあたかも会社のニーズを満たすためのロボットのようです。こんな環境にいつまで耐えていけるかわかりません。

I can't get ahead at a Japanese company where areas of responsibility are so fuzzy!!

> Do Japanese ever consider their own careers? Wouldn't it be better for them to do work that has personal responsibility and which means something for their own careers? They never become specialists in anything they do, but simply remain workers for their companies.

Foreigner's grievance: I work for a Japanese corporation that has a branch in America and recently, I was loaned to the Japanese headquarters for a two-year assignment.

However, my Japanese superiors hardly ever consider my career. They never listen to any of my requests about, for example, learning specialized skills or gaining particular knowledge. Instead, they always put the needs of the company first, assuming that we'll endure that in silence. In fact, looking closely, I see that my Japanese colleagues are all putting the needs of the company before their own careers too. Sometimes some of them have to **undergo reshuffles** because the company requires it, or they have to move from the sales section to the personnel section, etc. But they don't look as bothered about it as we would be. Why is this?

I am working in the company for my own career, so I want to do work where the area of my responsibility is made absolutely clear. I want to be engaged in something that uses my particular abilities—I don't want my area of responsibility left vague. That way, the division of work is made quite clear, and it makes it easier to do the job.

In Japanese organizations, the workers seem to be expected to be robots—they have to fulfill whatever needs the company has, and the areas of responsibility are left so vague. I don't know how long I can go on in this kind of situation.

日本人の反論　彼らはすぐに、自分のキャリアとか、自らの責任領域
だとかをうるさく言いますね。仕事ってそんな単純なものじゃない
でしょう。いろんな部署の動きが絡まり、お互いのニーズを調整し、
気を配りながら発展させていくものでしょう。

　そう、キャリアっていうのは、単なる計算能力や物を売る能力な
どではなく、内部組織のあらゆる状況を把握しながら、仕事を進め
ていける度量であり、力量を養うことだと思うんです。彼らは、そ
うしたことがわからず、ただ目先のキャリアにこだわるんです。だ
から、自分のやる仕事に線を引いてしまい、すぐにこれは私の責任
じゃないんですなんて言葉が口をついて出てしまう。**大人げないで
すよね。**

　彼らの言うように、自分のキャリアと守備範囲だけにこだわって
いたら、1塁と2塁の間にボールがきたらどうするんですか？ プロと
して育つということは、そうしたボールもうまく処理できるように
なることでしょう。こうした基本的なことを彼らは理解していない
のです。

分析

　日本人と欧米の人々との仕事に対する考え方の基本的な違いが、
自らのキャリアと会社のニーズとに関する価値観でしょう。欧米
の人は、自らが求める自分の将来像にそって、そのニーズに合っ
た仕事を求め、会社側と交渉します。そして、そこで合意したジ
ョブ・ディスクリプション（**業務内容**）に従って自らの仕事の領域
を決め、その範囲の中で自分の力量を発揮しようとします。

　それに対して、日本人は特に若手の場合、大学を卒業するとみ

Japanese retort: All those guys ever think about are their own careers, or their own areas of responsibility. Surely, a job involves so much more than that. Various departments facilitate their work, moving closely together, adjusting to each other's needs, and attending to many things.

In my opinion, having a "career" involves much more than merely the ability to sell or make a profit—it involves the capacity of mind and energy to get on with work while grasping all the various circumstances that prevail within an organization. But this is something they just don't understand—they're so bound up with thinking about their own careers and so make a sharp distinction between their sphere of work and that of others, and think nothing about declaring that such-and-such a task is none of their responsibility. It's so **immature**.

If people only think of their own careers, or sticking to their own particular areas of defense in the field, what happens when a ball comes in between first and second bases? Being a true professional surely involves being able to deal with balls that come between two bases, not straight at you. They don't even understand such a basic kind of thing.

Analysis

A fundamental difference between Japanese and Westerners' attitudes to work lies in the way of thinking about the relationship between one's own career and the company's needs. Westerners tend to pick jobs that accord with their idea of what they want to be in the future, and to negotiate with the company when they apply for a job. Both sides decide on a sphere of work for the individual according to a mutually agreed upon **job description**, and the person then has to show his or her capability within that sphere.

In contrast, when Japanese people join a company, especially if

な新人としてのスタートラインに並び、様々な経験やノウハウを有する会社に自らを育ててもらうというスタンスをとるのです。ですから、自らが求める業務と異なる部署に配属されても、それも教育の一環として甘受し、そうした経験を通してトータルな人格形成をしていこうとするのです。

したがって、日本人から見れば、やたら自らの責任とキャリアにこだわる欧米の人はわがままで子供っぽく見えるでしょうし、欧米の人から見れば、日本人はあたかも会社の奴隷か意思のないロボットのように見えるのです。

自らのキャリアを伸ばすことに忠実な欧米型の業務慣習にも、組織の様々なことに気を配りながら自分自身と業務とを同時に成長させていこうとする日本型の業務慣習にも、それぞれ長所もあれば短所もあるはずです。

1塁と2塁の間にきたボールを処理しながら、自らの人生を自らの力で伸ばしていける組織造りを行うには、2つの異なったビジネス文化の長所を取り合う柔軟性も必要になるのではないでしょうか。

ソリューション

❶ 欧米の人は、会社人間ではなく、個人のキャリア・アップを大切にする。個人の技能を伸ばしていくスタンスでのマネージメントが求められる。

❷ 職務内容をしっかりと決めて、責任領域をはっきりさせることからスタートしたい。その後は業績評価に至るまでのフィードバックをしっかりと。

❸ 国際企業では、業務の目標と個人のキャリア・アップの目標とが一致したとき組織が活性化する。常にお互いに評価し合う、まめな対応を心がけよう。

they are new recruits, or *shinjin*, they adopt a stance of getting the company to teach them all the know-how and expertise available there. Since this is the case, even if they are moved to another section, one where the work is different from the kind of work they want to do, they accept this as another stage in their education, and try to become total human beings through the experience.

Accordingly, from the Japanese point of view, Westerners who think only about their own careers or only want to do jobs for which they are personally responsible, seem selfish and childish. And from the Western point of view, the Japanese seem like company slaves, or robots with no opinions of their own.

But both approaches—both the Western model, where one tries determinedly to further one's own career, and the Japanese, where one tries to further oneself and the work at the same time, paying attention to various circumstances within the organization—have their good and bad points.

What is required is the flexibility to combine the good points of both business cultures even though they are so different so that companies and organizations can be built that allow people to develop their own lives with their own abilities, at the same time as being able to cover areas between first and second bases.

Solution

❶ Westerners are not "corporate soldiers." They place importance on advancing their own careers. Management should also take the approach of encouraging them to improve their technical skills.

❷ Start by deciding on clear job descriptions and clearly denote areas of responsibility. Next, provide steady feedback right down to performance evaluations.

❸ At international companies, when business goals and career objectives coincide, it invigorates the organization. Keep in mind that you should be receptive to constantlydoing detailed evaluations of one another.

日本の人事制度は差別の温床。とても耐えられなかったよ。

日本人は仕事で人を評価しない。あれこれ言っても年齢や、経歴、そして時にはどれくらい我慢したかなんて不思議なことで人を評価する。本当に不平等だよ。

外国人の不満　私は、オーストラリアで人事政策などを専門とする企業コンサルタント。実は若い頃に日本に留学して、日本企業で働いたことがあるんですが、結局数年で退職しました。それには、大きな理由があったんです。

日本人は自分たちはとても公平だという。でも、彼らの人事政策や人の評価の仕方を見ていると、決して頷けませんでした。

私には日本人の友人がいるのですが、彼はとても仕事ができて、優秀です。でも、彼は一向に昇進の機会を与えられません。理由はまだ若くて未経験だから。若いことが未経験と直結するこの発想は、私の国では**年齢に対する差別**と捉えられてもおかしくないんです。

優秀な人材ならば、その人の年齢や性別などといった背景にこだわらず、昇進や昇級の機会を与えるべきではないでしょうか。同じように、多くの日本人は私を外国人だからということで特別に扱っているような気がしてならないんです。

外国人という理由だけで**厚遇**され、最初はよかったなと思うんですが、次第にそれは彼らが私を仲間として受け入れていないからだなって思うようになりました。というのも、高給で優遇されてはいますが、決して会社の決裁に関係する中枢の業務には参画できないのです。人種に対する差別ですよねそれって。そんな文句がでると、

The Japanese personnel system is a breeding ground for discrimination. I couldn't stand it.

Japanese don't value the person at the workplace. No matter what they say, they put most store by age, background, and occasionally even things like how much a person has had to endure. I think it's really unfair.

Foreigner's grievance: I'm a corporate consultant in Australia specializing in things such as personnel policy. I actually studied abroad in Japan, and worked for a few years at a Japanese company, but I finally quit. There was a good reason for that.

The Japanese say that they are totally equal, but when I look at their personnel policies and the way they evaluate people, I really wonder.

I have a Japanese friend, and he is a really intelligent guy, good at his job, but he is never given the opportunity to rise in his company. The reason is that he is still young and lacks experience. This idea that you can necessarily link age with experience would be taken in my country as a kind of **age discrimination**.

If a person has superior talent, you shouldn't make any judgments based on things like age or sex, but give him or her the chance to rise—promote the person. Similarly, I can't help feeling that many Japanese give me special treatment simply because I'm a foreigner.

At first I enjoyed being given such **preferential treatment**, but gradually I started to think it was more because they didn't want to regard me as one of them. What I mean is, I get given special treatment and a higher salary, but I'm never allowed to participate in the inner decision-making processes that go on in the company. This is racial discrimination, isn't it? And if this complaint gets raised,

日本人はすぐにお金で解決しようとする。昇給に応じたりしてね。

　そんな対応を受けるたびに**疎外感**を覚えたものでした。そして結局会社をやめることにしたのです。

日本人の反論　私たちは常に人と人とのつながりを大切にするんです。いかにその人が仕事ができても、その人が若ければ、いきなり昇進させるわけにはいきません。そんなことをしたら、他の同僚との和が保てません。だいいち、若い頃にそんなふうに甘やかすことは、本人のためにもならないでしょう。いろんな苦労をして、単に仕事の技量だけではなく、人格的にも成長し、他の人からも認められてはじめて、それ相応の昇進の機会が与えられるべきだと思うんです。

　欧米の人にはそこのところがわからないんです。ただ、不平等だの機会均等に反しているなんて騒ぐのではなく、若い人に対する先輩の親心も大切にしてほしいのです。そうしたことが理解できて、本当に日本の社会にとけ込めれば、我々だって、どんどん外国人のことを受け入れますよ。でも彼らはそうじゃないでしょう。すぐ自分の国のことを引き合いに出して、我々の人事の方針や、伝統的な**上下関係**を批判するんです。

　日本の上下関係や、昇進制度には、人と人との和を重んじ、年月をかけて会社のためになる人格者を育てる知恵が隠されているんです。そこのところを理解してもらいたいものです。

the Japanese always try to solve it financially, by raising salaries and suchlike.

When I was treated like that, I felt really **alienated**. After that, I ended up quitting the company.

Japanese retort: We Japanese set great store by the relationships between people. No matter how good a person is at his or her job, if that person is young, there's no way you can suddenly let him or her rise to a high position at work. If you did that kind of thing, you'd never be able to keep a good atmosphere with colleagues at work. Firstly, if you spoiled someone so young in that way, it wouldn't be to the person's benefit. We think a person should undergo a certain amount of hardship and testing, and develop as a person as well as in his work abilities. When the person starts to be recognized for his or her abilities by other people, only then should he or she be given the opportunity to rise in the company.

This type of thing seems incomprehensible to Westerners. Instead of making such a fuss about conditions being unequal or being so contrary to "equal opportunity," I wish they would see the value of the kindness or parental feeling that older colleagues exercise toward their juniors. If only they could integrate themselves more in Japanese society, understanding this kind of thing, we would be more willing to accept them. But this seems to be beyond them. They're so quick to start comparing things with how they are in their own country, criticizing our personnel policies, or our traditional **seniority system**.

There is wisdom within Japan's seniority and promotion systems—a wisdom that sets great store by maintaining harmony between people, and developing people over a period of time so that they will become truly worthwhile members of the company. It would make things a whole lot easier if Westerners could understand this.

分析

　欧米型の平等の概念は、よく**機会に対する平等**と解釈されます。すなわち、年齢や性別、人種や国籍などに関係なく、あらゆる人にビジネス上の平等な機会が提供され、その機会に応え、よい結果をだした人は、どんどん昇進したり昇給したりできるというのが、機会に対する平等の概念です。この場合、求められている仕事での実績だけが、評価の対象になるのです。

　それに対して、かなり変わってきたとはいえ、日本をはじめとしたアジアのいくつかの国では、機会に対する平等以上に、その人が社会でどのように評価され、受け入れられているかという点に評価の基準が集まりがちです。それは時には、その人の人生経験を積んできた事の証明である年齢であり、場合によってはそれまでの**学歴**であり、時には**家柄**や社内での人望という、実務での成果とは異なった評価基準であったりします。

　こうした考え方の違いの背景には、他の人と同質であることに価値の基準をおく文化と、他人と違うこと、際立つことをよしとする文化との確執があるようです。

　日本では、ある時点までは、他の人と協調して、他の人の状況を理解しながら、グループの一員として成長することをよしとします。そして、その過程を経てはじめてより大きな責任ある地位を勝ち得ていくのです。
　したがって、そんな日本人からアメリカ人を見たならば、単に目先の仕事のみで人を評価している様子が**軽率**にすら思えてきます。しかし逆に、欧米の人がそんな日本の社会を見るならば、人

Analysis

The American concept of equality is often interpreted to mean **equality regarding opportunity**. That is to say, equal business opportunities for everyone, without regard to age, gender, ethnicity, or nationality. Those who respond to the opportunity and show good results should be allowed to rise high in the world and better themselves—this is the concept of "equal opportunity." In such a situation, what comes under scrutiny and evaluation is solely a person's actual achievements in the work for which a position is being sought.

By contrast, although it is gradually changing, in many Asian countries, especially Japan, over and above equality of opportunity, the standards tend to focus around the issue of how a particular person may be evaluated or accepted by society. And this may be a matter of a person's age, which demonstrates that he or she has accumulated a certain amount of life experience, or occasionally it can be his or her **educational record**; or sometimes it may be his or her **family background** or popularity within the company. All of these contribute to a slightly different scale of evaluation from solely the individual's performance "on the job."

Behind this divergence in thought is probably the difference of opinion between two different cultures, one of which places value on being the same as, or homogenous with, other people, and one that sees being different from other people and standing out as a good thing.

In Japan, it is thought to be a good thing if, at least for a while, one blends with other people and grows as a member of a group, trying to understand the circumstances of everyone else in the group. Only when one has gone through a certain process or course can one finally achieve a position that has rather greater responsibility.

Accordingly, to the Japanese, the way Americans seem to make evaluations of people merely from present performance seems somewhat **imprudent**. Conversely, seen through American eyes, Japanese society seems like a society in which people are **bound hand**

の能力を画一的に判断し評価する、**がんじがらめ**の社会に思える
ことでしょう。

　どちらも一長一短、どのような文化にも、強い側面と弱い側面
とがあるわけで、ついついお互いの弱い面だけが見えてしまうの
が、異文化でのコミュニケーションの落とし穴なのです。

ソリューション

❶ 欧米流の人事制度を習得し理解することから、グローバルな組織造りはス
タートする。基本は個人をその背景で評価せず、その時点での成績や将来
性で評価すること。

❷ 公平と平等とは根本的に異なる概念。人を性別や年齢、人種、障害の有無
などを理由とせずにスタートラインに並べることが平等。これはEqual
Opportunityといって、欧米の人事政策の骨幹となっている。

❸ 本人の希望やニーズこそがスタートラインにいかにつくかの条件になる。
それから先は本人次第。その羅針盤となるのがフィードバックや業績評価
なのだ。

and foot, one in which judgments and evaluations of people's ability are made in a very narrow and fixed way.

But both ways have their merits and demerits, and there are strong and weak sides to any culture. Merely to let the weak side of the other's culture dominate one's view is to fall into a trap inherent in communication with a culture that is altogether different to one's own.

Solution

❶ By understanding and learning the Western personnel system, you can start to build a global organization. It is fundamental that rather than evaluating someone based on the person's background, one should use his or her present performance and potential.

❷ Fairness and equality are fundamentally different concepts. Equality means that people line up at the starting line without discrimination based on gender, age, race, disabilities, etc. This is known as equal opportunity and is a fundamental part of personnel policy.

❸ It is a person's hopes and needs that determine his or her starting line. After that, it is up to the person. Feedback and performance evaluations are your compass.

グローバルに
なれない日本人

ROUND **4**

**Japanese Problems with
Being "Global"**

日本の特殊性だって?!
もう耳にタコができたよ。

世界中で、日本ぐらい自分の特殊性にこだわる国はありません。いつも日本が同意しないので、物事がややこしくなるんです。

外国人の不満 　私は、デンマーク人。ニューヨークに住んでいるときに製薬会社に就職して、その後日本の担当として東京にやってきました。東京は魅力的な町で、毎日楽しく暮らしています。でも、仕事の上では、日本人の頑固な対応に閉口させられることがしばしばです。

　日本人は口を開ければ自分たちには特殊な事情があると言います。**商習慣**が特別だとか、消費者の趣向が特別だとか、**あげくの果て**には日本そのものが他とは違ったユニークな国だとくるからたまりません。

　どこの国だってユニークですよ。何も日本だけじゃない。どんな国にも特殊な事情があり、固有の文化があるのに、どうして日本人だけがあんなに自分の事情にこだわるのでしょうか。

　私の会社では、日本だけが独自のコマーシャルを使用して商品を販売していますし、その仕様だって日本向けだけに特別なデザインを施している。これは世界規模で見たとき、余分なコストを使っていることになるわけです。こんなことをしていると日本は本当に孤立してしまいますよ。

日本人の反論 　我々はもっと彼らに日本のことを勉強してほしいんですよ。我々は、他の国と違っていかにうるさい消費者と対応してい

I'm tired of hearing about Japanese uniqueness.

> No other country in the world is so obsessed as Japan with its own uniqueness. It's always the Japanese who hold matters up and insist on their own way of doing things.

Foreigner's grievance: I'm from Denmark. I was hired by a pharmaceutical company while living in New York, and later, I was sent to Tokyo and put in charge of the Japan office. Tokyo has a lot of charm, and I enjoy living here. At work, however, I'm frequently frustrated by Japanese stubbornness.

I can't stand it the way every time the Japanese open their mouths, it's to claim there's something special or unique about circumstances in Japan. Either it's Japanese **commercial practices** that are special, or Japanese consumers' tastes that are so particular—and in the end, **to top it all off**, they resort to saying that Japan itself is a unique country and quite unlike any other country in the world.

Every country in the world is "unique"—not only Japan. Every country has its own characteristic conditions and its own particular culture. Why is it that only the Japanese are so **obsessed with** their own specialness and uniqueness?

In my company, only Japan has to have its own commercials to sell the products. Even the appearance of the products has to be designed especially to appeal to Japanese tastes. If this were done on a worldwide scale, think of the extra costs it would entail. If Japan carries on this way, it's going to find itself cut off in its own little world.

Japanese retort:

Those guys should do a little research and find out just how much more fussy in fact the consumers are that we have to deal with in

るかってことを。実際、彼らのいうグローバル・スタンダードに則った商品を持ち込んで、それで成功するなら、どんなに楽か。

海外とは比較にならない速度で新製品のデザインが変化し、商品の微妙な仕様がその商品の運命を決定的に決めてしまう。しかも、日本の競合企業は、我々に打ち勝つために夜も寝ずに開発に取り組んでいるんです。だいいち、中途半端な商品であれば、小売店も取次業者も見向きもしませんよ。

彼らの商品は実用的かもしれないが、我々からすれば**繊細じゃない**。細かいところへの気配りがない。しかも、アフターケアが十分じゃない。

そうした問題点を我々は一身に背負って解決しようとしているんです。彼らに日本のマーケットの特殊性への理解が少しでもあれば、もっともっと得意客をつかむことができるんですがね。

■ 分析

両者の言い分には、それぞれ一理も二理もあります。確かに、日本の消費者はうるさいでしょうし、他の国ではあり得ないような細かい要求をしてくるかもしれません。特に、長年にわたって様々なインフラを完成させてきた日本では、そのインフラに合致したデザインで商品を製造しなければならないというケースもあるでしょう。

また、コマーシャルひとつにしても、日本人の**テイストに合った**ものを制作する必要性はよく理解できます。日本の成熟したマーケットに向けて競争力のある商品を開発することは確かに並大抵のことではないでしょう。

しかし、だからと言って、外国人の不満が**的外れ**かというとそ

Japan—they're much more particular than customers in other countries. No one would be happier if those guys could actually make a success in Japan with those goods that have, as they say, met "global standards."

They've got to understand that in Japan product designs change at a speed to which the rate in other countries just doesn't compare. And often a slight detail in the appearance of a product has a decisive effect on its fate. Furthermore, competitor enterprises in Japan are busily developing new products, working day and night in order to try to get the better of us. Most importantly, if the product isn't state of the art, neither retailers nor distributors will bother even to look at it.

To us, those guys' products might be practical, but they're so **unwieldy**; and often insufficient attention has been paid to the details. Moreover, the "aftercare"—the back-up service after the sale—they provide just isn't good enough.

These are the kinds of things we take it upon ourselves to see to and solve. If they had even the slightest understanding of the particular conditions of the market in Japan, they would be able to get so many more clients than they have now.

Analysis

Here, the assertion of each side has its own particular grain of truth. Certainly, Japanese consumers are very fussy: they do make demands that would be unheard of in any other country. Particularly, in as much as Japan has managed to perfect its various forms of infrastructure over many years, there probably is the general expectation in Japan that manufactured products should reflect that infrastructure.

And again, as far as the matter of commercials is concerned, it's understandable that the Japanese should feel the necessity to produce commercials that **speak to the tastes of** Japanese people. It is no small endeavor to develop and sell goods with competitive power that appeal to the sophisticated Japanese market.

However, this doesn't mean that what the non-Japanese is saying

うでもありません。日本側も単に自分たちの事情を強調して文句
ばかり言うのではなく、日本向けの商品を開発するために、チー
ムの一員として彼らを迎えるべく努力したいものです。それには、
まず相手にやる気を起こしてもらわなければなりません。いかに
日本のマーケットが魅力的で、その果実を獲得するには、何が必
要かというふうに、前章でも触れたベネフィットを強調し、相手
に協力を求めるスタンスが必要です。

　日本人は、得てしてマーケットからのプレッシャーが大きいせ
いか、マーケット側に立って、自分の会社や外国人の同僚を批判
してしまう傾向があります。実際に、外資系企業の中で、日本人
は消費者の味方なのか、それとも我が社の社員なのかという疑念
が、外国人の重役たちの間でささやかれているのです。あくまで
も会社の一員として、外国人の同僚と一緒になって、日本のマー
ケットで成功するよう、方策を練っていく必要があるのです。

　同時に、外国人も、そうした日本のマーケットを単に本社から
操ろうとするのではなく、できるだけ機会を見つけて日本の実際
の市場に触れるよう努力すべきでしょう。

ソリューション

❶ 日本の特殊性だけを強調しても何も益なし。外資系企業に働く日本人は、
自分が日本の顧客サイドに立って仕事をして、自らの本社のニーズへの同
情や忠誠が欠如していないか常にチェックしよう。

❷ 確かに、日本のマーケットは複雑で、顧客のニーズは細かい。でもそれを
克服すればフルーツも大きい。海外のパートナーに文句をいうのではなく、
フルーツの大きさを強調して、一緒にマーケットに臨むスタンスを養おう。

❸ 海外のパートナーを阻害するな。彼らと共に日本のマーケットを開発でき
てこそ、真の強い組織が育まれる。

here is completely **off the mark**. Instead of the Japanese side just stressing and complaining about the special conditions it has to face, they should try instead to work together as a team in developing goods that will appeal to the Japanese market. And for this, above all, what is necessary is the desire to try. The right kind of attitude to present would be to seek their cooperation, emphasizing how attractive the market is, and asking what they think you should do to reap the benefits of that market—putting the emphasis on the positive aspects, as I explained in the previous chapter.

Japanese often do have a tendency, perhaps because of the pressure they feel from their own market, to stand on the side of that market and to criticize their own companies or their foreign colleagues. In fact, in foreign corporations the people in executive positions do sometimes wonder privately amongst themselves whether the Japanese working for them are really working for them, or for their own Japanese consumers. So it is vital that you show yourself to be a member of the company and join your foreign colleagues in developing policies that will help products succeed in the Japanese market.

At the same time, the foreigners shouldn't just try to manipulate the market in Japan from the main company in the States, but should make every effort to find the opportunity to actually see the Japanese market for themselves.

Solution

❶ There is no benefit in emphasizing the uniqueness of Japan. Japanese who work at foreign-owned companies should always check that they are working on the side of the Japanese customer and are not lacking in sympathy and loyalty to the needs of the head office.

❷ The Japanese market is certainly complicated, and the customers are picky. However, if you overcome these obstacles the bounties are large. Do not complain to your foreign partners. Emphasize the size of the bounties and take the approach of dealing with the market together.

❸ Do not be an obstacle to your foreign partners. If you work with them to develop the Japanese market, you can build a strong organization.

事例

25

なんで日本人だけを信用するんだい？
僕たちはいつもかやの外……

> 日本企業の取引先は現地法人の日本人といつも一緒に行動する。そして、現地の社員と交流しようとしない。現地の社員は単なるお飾りのようだ。そんな日本人の対応に不満が蓄積されている。

外国人の不満　僕はアメリカで日系企業につとめている。取引先は同じくアメリカに進出している日系企業。でもね、ときどき、先方のアメリカ人の営業マンとランチをしながら愚痴をこぼすんです。

　というのも、大切なことはいつも僕の日本人の上司と取引先の日本人担当者との間でコーディネートされてしまう。いつだったか、本社から日本人の営業関係者がやってきて、その取引先のところに一緒に行ったんだけど、先方も日本人の担当者を出してきて、何から何まで2人で話してしまうんです。しかも多くは日本語でね。長々と日本語で話したあと、簡単な英語でちょっと通訳してくれるだけ。

　我々がいろいろと意見を言っても、そうだねって**おざなりに対応**するだけで、また日本人同士で話し込んでしまう。僕たちは単なるお飾りなんだねって、向こうのアメリカ人担当者と話したものでした。
　いくら相手が日系の企業だって、ここはアメリカでしょ。アメリカのことをよく理解している我々にどうして仕事を任せてくれないんでしょうか。これは**侮辱**です。

Why do Japanese people only trust other Japanese? We're always regarded as outsiders.

> Japanese clients always interact with other Japanese people in branch companies abroad—and they never have anything to do with the local people in the companies. The local workers seem more like symbolic decorations. A lot of resentment and dissatisfaction builds up when the Japanese treat people like this.

Foreigner's grievance: I work for a Japanese corporation in the United States, and the clients are likewise all Japanese who have branched out and launched companies in America. But sometimes I have lunch with other American sales reps employed in these other companies, and we complain to each other about the way things are handled.

What gets me is the way that anything important always gets decided by my Japanese superior and the Japanese person who's handling matters for the client company. Some while ago, a guy involved in operations came over from the head office in Japan, and the two of us went to visit a Japanese client company together. But the company sent out a Japanese to deal with us, and the two of them just decided everything, from start to finish, between themselves. Nearly all of the discussion was carried on in Japanese. After long exchanges, they would follow with just a short explanation in English.

We give various opinions on matters, but all they do is reply **perfunctorily** to me with "Yes, quite," and then carry on talking to each other. I had a chat with my counterpart from the other company, an American, about this, and we agreed: we American workers are nothing but decorations, with purely symbolic value.

Okay, so it's a Japanese company—but this is America, isn't it? Why don't they let us handle the job? We're the ones who know about things in this country. It's **humiliating**.

実はね、一度シンガポールに出張したとき、向こうの営業の人と意見交換したことがあったんですが、彼らも同じ苦情を言っていましたよ。なぜ日本人は日本人しか信用しないんでしょう？

日本人の反論　我々は別にアメリカ人を信用していないわけじゃないんです。あの取引先は我々にとっては古くからの大切なお客さんで、日本では本社同士で大変深い交流を持っています。我々が彼らのために製造している部品だって、彼らの日本の工場の技術者と**綿密に打ち合わせ、検討を重ねた**上でアメリカに持ってきているのです。

だから、ここがいかにアメリカとはいえ、日本での業務の関係をも含めた繊細な話をしなければならないわけで、そうした事情をアメリカ人の従業員もわかってほしいんです。

だいいち、そんな本支社間の事情を彼らがすべて理解して、営業的な対応ができるようになるまでには、相当な時間と訓練が必要でしょう。だから、もうちょっと**ねばり強く**我慢して経験を積んでほしいんですがね。

彼らはすぐ目先のことで文句を言うんです。そして意見が合わなかったらすぐに辞めてしまう。そんなことだから、いつまでたっても日本人がすべてを処理しなければならなくなるんです。

いったいいつになったら、彼らに本当に仕事を任せることができるようになるんでしょうか？

In fact, when I went on a business trip to Singapore, I swapped stories with some guys working for a Japanese company there, and they had exactly the same complaint. Why do the Japanese only trust other Japanese?

Japanese retort: It's not that we have difficulty trusting Americans. The customer involved in the above case happened to be a particularly important long-standing client of ours, that's all; our head offices in Japan have a very deep relationship. The machine parts we make for them here in America are made only after **intense prior discussions** with technicians at their factories in Japan, and **much experimentation and testing**.

So even though this might be America, there are many intricate matters we simply have to talk about, including, among other things, matters that have to do with our operations with them in Japan. If the Americans would only understand this kind of thing.

In any case, think how much experience and training are necessary to really appreciate the relations between the main office and various branch companies, and to conduct business appropriately. For this reason, we wish they would **hang in there** with a little more patience until they gain experience.

They're so quick to complain about a situation as it strikes them. And when they don't get what they demand right then and there—well, they just up and leave! It's because they do this that the Japanese feel they can't let go of responsibility and have to keep charge of everything.

We would like to be able to let them handle a job by themselves, but we just don't see when that time will ever come.

分析

いかに現地の支社に技術を移管して、しかもその技術にリンクした顧客サービスを展開するかについては、どの国際企業でも最も悩んでいることです。

特に、古くからの関係を重んじる日本企業の場合、海外に進出しても日本での関係に頼って、日本人の担当者同士のコミュニケーションに依存してしまう傾向が強いようです。

問題は、そうした課題をいかにオープンに現地社員に話し、技術を移管するプログラムを共同で作り上げ、目標に向かってチームワークが組めるかということでしょう。

次項でも触れますが、技術移管のプログラムを組むとき、日本人はとかく数年、時には10年以上の長期間にわたる大目標を掲げ、現地の人に提示します。それに対して、特にアメリカ人の場合、より具体的な目に見える目標を求めようとします。この感覚の違いが時には更なる誤解の原因となるのです。

階段を一歩一歩踏みしめるような形で、双方の協力体制を構築するスタンスが必要です。そして、取引先に対応するときも、日本の取引先の事情を説明した上で、事情に合致した人材の投入を行うべきです。マネージャーやディレクターとして採用した人が、日本人同士の打ち合わせの外におかれるのは好ましくありません。むしろ、日本人の部下の上にそうした人材をおいて機能できるよう、人的な投資を急ぐべきです。

現地法人を成長させるためには、初期の準備期間の後に、でき

Analysis

The problem here involves issues surrounding how best to transfer skills and technology to branch companies abroad and how to develop customer service that is linked to that technology. This is a knotty issue, one that every international enterprise has difficulty with.

Japanese corporations, particularly since they place such value on long-standing relationships, do have a tendency, even after they have made inroads into other countries, to rely on the links they made with companies in Japan, and to depend too heavily on communication carried out between Japanese workers rather than local people.

The problem lies in how best to talk to the local company people openly about these issues so that a program can be jointly constructed that will allow technology to be transferred—so that people from both sides can work as a team toward the same goal.

I'll refer to this in the next case, but often when Japanese put together a program for transfer of technology and skills, they hold up long-term objectives meant to span several years (sometimes as many as ten, or even longer) to the people at the branch company. But most foreigners, especially Americans, will want a more **tangible objective**. This difference in sensibilities can sometimes become the cause of yet more misunderstanding.

You have to be willing to construct a system that allows each side to cooperate with the other—to progress slowly, one step at a time. And in dealing with Japanese clients, you should try to invest a little in human resources—employ the kind of person who can handle the job, who will be able to handle the situation with the Japanese customers once you have explained it. It is not a good thing to have someone you employed in a managerial position left out of discussions held entirely among Japanese. Rather, you should place this sort of person in charge of Japanese subordinates, in a position where he or she can utilize his or her full potential.

To help your overseas branches maximize their potential, after

るだけ早く現地法人に**自主性**を与え、現地の従業員のやる気を高めなければならないことは言うまでもありません。

　日本人が**院政**をしいて、現地法人を操るような構造は早く改めるべきでしょう。

ソリューション

❶ 日本の顧客のニーズを具体的にわかりやすく欧米のパートナーに伝えよう。そしてパートナーも交えて、試行錯誤を繰り返そう。

❷ 日本企業よ、海外の支店に表向きだけ権限を与えて、結局本社が院政を敷くようなマネージメントは改めよう。多様な環境での全員参加こそ、グローバル企業に成長するステップなのだ。

❸ 難しい日本の取引先と欧米のパートナーとの間に立つときこそ、双方のビジネス文化に精通した人材を発掘して、投資しよう。

the initial period of preparation it's obvious that you have to give local people as much **autonomy** as possible in order to increase their motivation.

There is a need for some urgent restructuring of the system as it has existed up till now, where local workers are hired but the Japanese remain a "**hidden power behind the throne.**"

Solution

❶ Explain the needs of Japanese customers using specifics in an easy to understand way to your Western partners. Then, with your partner, practice over and over, learning through trial and error.

❷ Refrain from using a management style in which power is officially transferred to the local office abroad, and the headquarters Is a hidden power behind the throne. An important step to becoming a global company is to let all the people from various business environments join.

❸ When you are between your foreign partners and picky Japanese customers, find and hire personnel who are acquainted with the business cultures of both.

事例 26

日本人よ、どこまで任せてくれるの？
しっかりとした方針を決めてほしい。

日本人は極端なんだよ。管理するとなれば、箸の上げ下ろしまでとやかく言うし、いったん任せるとなれば、今度は何も言ってこない。もっと状況に応じて柔軟に対応したらどうなんだ！

外国人の不満 　私の会社はシカゴにあって、日本の会社が出資しています。以前は窒息しそうなほどに、日本からの駐在員に細かいところまで管理され、うるさく指導され、多くの現地社員が辞めていきました。何度も悲しい訴訟まで体験しました。

　そんな苦しみの中から、現地のことは現地の人が最もよく知っているので、思い切って任せてはということになったんです。するとどうでしょう、最初は与えられた自由の中でのびのびと仕事ができたんです。ところがこのごろ、だんだん不安になってきたんです。この会社がどこに向かおうとしているのか、我々にはわからないんです。そして、我々が会社にどのように貢献しているのかが見えなくなってしまったんです。

　我々は結局、日本の本社から見れば単なる一地域の支局にすぎないんだって思うようになりました。ただ放り出されて、無秩序なまま放置されているやっかいものではないのかってね。

　私はこの会社がここに支社をつくったころからずっと勤めています。すべてを任せられてしまったけれど、本社からの指導もないまま、大きなミスをしでかしたり、不良品を製造してしまったりしたらど

Mr. Japanese! How much are you going to leave up to us? Decide on a firm policy!

> The Japanese are either one extreme or the other. When they supervise, they interfere in the tiniest thing. But when they give a job over to you to do, they leave everything entirely up to you and offer no help at all. What about showing a little flexibility from time to time?!

Foreigner's grievance: My company in Chicago is financed by a Japanese corporation. Previously, it was **almost suffocating** the way we were supervised and told what to do by Japanese people from the main company in Japan, even in the tiniest detail. Many of the workers here couldn't stand it and left. There were a number of difficult court cases.

Because we had such a difficult time of it, the suggestion was made that since the people working here in the subsidiary company understand what's going on around here best, the corporation should go ahead and give them full responsibility for everything. Well, at first it was okay; we got on with the job, enjoying the newly acquired freedom. But I've started to get worried recently—I mean, we have no idea of the basic policy of this corporation—and no idea of whether what we do actually makes any contribution.

I've started to think that as far as the head office in Japan is concerned, we're simply a subsidiary, an unimportant branch office in a provincial region—maybe we're just a **nuisance**, and have just been let go. Maybe we're just going to be allowed to go to ruin.

I've been working for this Japanese corporation ever since it first set up the branch company here. We've been given full responsibility, yes, but with no directives coming from the main office. It's worrying; who knows if we're doing something wrong, something that's really

うしようかって、不安でなりません。我々は**求心力**を持たない無秩序な組織になってしまうのではないでしょうか?

日本人の反論　本当に海外での組織運営は難しいですね。技術移管をするには厳しく指導しなければならないことだってあるでしょう。でも、厳しく接すれば接するほど、現地の人の心は離れていく。我々の親心を理解してもらえないばかりか、時にはちょっとした誤解が原因で訴訟問題にまで発展してしまう。

　だから、海外でのマネージメントについていろいろと研究し、思い切って現地の人に任せてみることにしたんです。権限を**委譲**せよといろんな本にも書いているでしょ。

　とはいえ、いざそうしてみると、今度は現地の状況がまったく摑めなくなる。我々は高い目標を設定したんです。現地の人に任せることによって、現地での生産力を大幅にアップさせるってね。

　ところが、最近現地で頻繁にミスが起きています。品質管理が充分でなく、その結果取引先に迷惑をかける事故も起き、売上も**横這**い状態です。いったい何に問題があるんでしょうか?

分析

　最近、権限委譲という言葉がよく語られます。現地のことは現地に任せて、彼らの創意工夫を引き出し、やる気をだしてもらおうというわけです。この考え方自体悪いことではありません。ただ、ここにいくつかの条件があることを忘れないようにしましょう。

bad for the company, or if the goods we're producing are deficient in some way. Are we going to be allowed to just collapse, with no **centralizing force** holding us together?

Japanese retort: You can't win when you run a business overseas, can you? For example, in transfer of technology and skills, sometimes you have to be really tough and demanding when you show people the ropes. But the tougher we are with the guys over there, the more angry and alienated they get. Not only do they not understand that we're being strict out of kind intentions—sometimes we even find ourselves being hauled up in court because of something that has arisen out of a small misunderstanding.

This is why, after doing some research on management overseas, we simply gave everything over to the non-Japanese in our subsidiary company overseas. That's what it said in the books—that it's best to **hand over** complete control.

But now that we've done that, we no longer have any idea of what's going on over there. We set a high objective; we assumed that by leaving the running of the company completely up to the local people, productivity would increase markedly.

But recently masses of errors have been occurring over there. The product quality control is deficient, and as a result, mishaps occur that cause great inconvenience to our clients—so our total sales are beginning to **slack off**. What can the problem be?

Analysis

The phrase "transfer of authority" is one we've been hearing a lot recently. The idea is that by leaving decisions up to local people in the Japanese companies overseas, this will stimulate their creativity, imagination, and determination to do their best. It's not a bad idea in itself, but we shouldn't forget that a number of conditions are necessary for it to work.

　まず、本社と現地とが共同の目標をもって、常にチームワークを創造しているかを確認する必要があります。その目標には2種類あります。まず、**必ず実現可能な目に見える目標を設定すること**です。日本のビジネス文化には、一見達成不可能にみえる大きな目標を設定し、あとは個々の努力に期待する傾向があります。

　一方で大きな理想は明解に掲げながらも、常に達成可能な目標を視野に入れるという両輪が必要なのです。特に、技術移管の初期の段階では、欧米の人にはその目標に対して彼らがどれだけ近づき、さらにどのような工夫が必要かといった具体的なフィードバックが欠かせないことは、既に説明したはずです。

　大切なことは、**結果を重視**し、プロセスの選択にはできるだけ自由を与えるということをここで再度強調しておきましょう。

　そして、次に大事なことは、本当に現地に権限を委譲するなら、本社にも現地に協力できる様々な機構をつくることです。そのためには、世界中から人を選び、本社の中枢部で昇進させるぐらいの深みを持った人事政策を実施したいものです。

　そのことによって、任せっぱなしではなく、お互いが大切なパートナーであるということを両者ともに実感できるのです。

　現地に任せるということは、将軍が大名を任命するように、本社から現地組織に自治を与えることではないのです。

　少なくともビジネスの現場においては、本社、現地といった上下関係を払拭して、お互いに平等なパートナーシップを創造するようにしなければなりません。円滑なコミュニケーションと人的

First of all, the head office and the branch offices overseas must make sure that they share the same objectives and that they are working in a way that encourages teamwork. There are two qualities that the objectives should have. First and foremost, they have to be **tangible and achievable**. Japanese corporate culture has a tendency to set up huge objectives, ones that it is quite obvious will never be reached, and just hope that everyone will put in the right kind of effort regardless.

While clearly promoting these larger ideals, it is also necessary always to make clear that these objectives are being reached. Particularly in the early stages of technology transfer, as I've already explained, it is vital to give specific feedback to non-Japanese nationals working for you, telling them things like how close they have come to achieving those objectives, and what further endeavors are necessary.

The important thing, I should stress one more time, is to **place value on the results** and to give as much freedom as possible to the selection process.

Next, if you are truly going to confer autonomy on the company overseas, it is important to set up various mechanisms that will allow the head office and the overseas branch to cooperate with each other.

And for this, it is a good thing to exercise effective personnel policies that will allow you to select non-Japanese to rise in the inner circles of the main company. It is through this kind of effort that both sides will be able to truly feel that they are partners engaged in a mutual project, and that one side is not just being left to get on with things alone.

Letting local subsidiaries of the company take charge is not just a matter of the head company giving autonomy to local organizations and letting them get on with things alone in the same way the shogun appointed local lords, to govern domains in the old days.

At least in the corporate workplace, we should get rid of the hierarchy between the head company and overseas branches, aiming for a partnership with mutual equality. A **unilateral** transfer of authority without adequate communication and harmonious exchange is a bad

交流の不足した**一方的な権限委譲**は、組織としての求心力を無視した最も危険な選択でもあるのです。

ソリューション

❶ 国際企業においては、組織も個人と一緒。常にフィードバックをし、意見交換して目標に導き合う姿勢が欠かせない。

❷ 権限委譲をするには、目に見える具体的な目標の設定と合意が必要不可欠。長期目標だけでなく、ステップごとのゴールを設定して権限委譲に取り組もう。そして常にお互いのニーズに耳を傾け、建設的なコミュニケーションにつとめよう。

❸ 組織がまだ幼いときの過大な権限委譲は逆効果。組織の発育を促すためのノウハウを会社に植え付けよう。

move for any organization, one that basically ends up destroying what holds a company together.

Solution

❶ At an international company, the organization and the individual are one and the same. Constantly giving feedback and an maintaining an attitude of achieving goals through an exchange of ideas is indispensable.

❷ When delegating authority, it is essential to establish and agree upon clearly visible, concrete goals. Make an effort to establish not just long-term goals, but set goals for each step, and make an effort to delegate authority.

❸ Delegating too much authority while the organization is still young will backfire. Make sure to implant the knowhow to steer the organization's growth in the company.

日本人よ、グローバルだよ、グローバル!!
あなたたちは孤立したいのかい?

> グローバル・スタンダードって言うとどうして日本人はむっとするんだろうか。日本人は外国と歩調を合わせようとしないばかりか、そうした必要性を強調しても、協力はおろか、頑なに自分の殻にとじこもってしまうんだ。

外国人の不満　僕は企業の収益性をアップすることを目指した国際ビジネスコンサルタント。日本にも顧客がいて、海外との取引についていろんな相談を受けています。

日本人は、我々がもっとグローバルに対応してほしいというと、表面上は了解したような応対をするんだ。でも、実際は何も変えないばかりか、むしろもっと**頑固**に自分のやり方を守ろうとする。口では国際化の必要性を唱えているけど、それは単なる**お題目**で、本当は海外とは文字どおり「海の向こうのこと」で、できれば日本に持ち込みたくないのではないだろうか。

しかし、このままでは日本は本当に孤立してしまうと思うんだ。もっと、心を開いて海外のものを受け入れ、自らも情報を提供していかなければ、日本は孤立した扱いにくい国として多くの人から敬遠されてしまうよ。

日本人の反論　彼らのいうグローバル・スタンダードって、本当の国際感覚に基づいているとは思えないんです。

私の仕事の相手はアメリカなんですけどね。彼らがグローバル・スタンダードって言うとき、それは結局のところアメリカン・スタンダードにすぎず、アメリカのやり方を押しつけてきているだけの

Mr. Japanese! The world is globalizing. Globalizing!! Do you want to isolate yourselves?

> Why do the Japanese always get miffed at the mention of "global standards"? The Japanese don't make any effort to fit in with the pace of other countries, and when you stress the necessity for this, far from cooperating, they simply retreat stubbornly further back into their shell.

Foreigner's grievance: I'm an international business consultant for companies that are trying to improve their profitability. I have clients in Japan, and consult with them about overseas transactions.

When we tell the Japanese that we want them to treat matters more globally, they always respond in a manner that seems on the surface to indicate that they have understood us. But in reality, far from making any changes to what they practice, they try all the more **stubbornly** to preserve their own way of doing things. Verbally, they all preach about the necessity of "internationalization," but that's just **empty talk**. Really, everything they do with other countries is literally something that happens "over there," "far away." They would prefer if possible not to let it have any effect on anything that happens in Japan.

If this carries on, I really think Japan is going to end up isolated. If they don't open up more, accept things from other countries, and offer information themselves, Japan is going to end up being sidestepped by most countries and seen as an isolated, idiosyncratic nation.

Japanese retort: I just can't accept that the "global standards" they go on about are actually based on an international sensibility.

The guys I work with are Americans. When they say "global standards," I get the feeling that what this means is simply "American standards," and it's just a way of forcing us to follow their way of doing

ような気がするんです。アメリカのやり方をグローバルだと思って外国に押しつけようとする彼らの**自惚れと無神経さ**に腹が立つんです。

本当にグローバルにと言うならば、むしろ世界各国の事情を理解して、お互いの特殊性を尊重しながら協力できる方向を探るべきでしょう。

彼らは国内ではやれそれぞれの国や人種の多様性を尊重しようなどと言っているくせに、いったん国を離れると、すべてアメリカの常識に一元化しようとする。こうした**都合の良さ**に我々は耐えられないんです。きっと日本だけではなく、多くの国の人々も同じように思っているんじゃないでしょうか。

分析

他国の事情をその国の常識に則って理解し行動するということは簡単ではないのです。ここでは、日本人の指摘に共感できる一面、実は海外における日本人も同じように日本の常識を尺度にしてその国の人やビジネス文化を批判しているケースが山ほどあるということを知っておくべきです。そうした批判は、アメリカに進出している日系企業に働くアメリカ人をはじめ、世界各国からあがっています。

そうです。お互いにお互いの**横柄さ**を批判しながら、実は「**蟹の横這い**」のように、同じ失敗を繰り返しているのです。

人間は、自分の生活している環境から強い影響を受けて育ちます。そして、理屈の上では相手は違った文化や環境に育っているということは理解できても、ビジネスなどの現場でコミュニケーションがうまくいかないと、やはりその原因を相手に求めてしまうのです。

things. I get furious at their **arrogance and insensitivity**, at the way they think American ways are "global" and try to force them on other countries.

A truly "global" way of going about matters would be to look for a way in which, showing understanding of the conditions in various countries around the world, we could cooperate, respecting each other's uniqueness.

They're always touting the multiculturalism within America that allows them to respect each other's countries of origin and ethnicity, but let them get out of the country, and they try to make everybody else conform to what America sees as acceptable. It's this **hypocrisy** of theirs that we can't stand. It's not only Japan that thinks this way—lots of countries all over the world do too, I'm sure.

Analysis

To try to objectively understand the conditions of other countries, and to take action accordingly is no easy task. While I can sympathize with the comments of the Japanese in this case, the fact is, Japanese people all too often do the same thing—criticize corporate culture in other countries using the yardstick of what is commonly accepted or common practice in Japan. This criticism is often heard from Americans working for Japanese enterprises who have set up companies in the United States, and in fact in various countries all around the world.

That's right. Even though we each criticize what we see as the other's **arrogance**, in fact, we often do the exact same thing ourselves—just like **a crab that can only crawl sideways**.

Human beings are strongly influenced by the environments in which they grow up and live. And even when they can understand on a theoretical level that another person has come from another culture and environment, when communication fails—for example, in a corporate situation—they often look for the cause in the other person.

　ここでは、グローバル・スタンダードとはいったい何を意味しているのかを考えるべきです。それぞれの国の実状を無視してスタンダードを設定するのではなく、どのようなビジネスを世界で展開したいのか、その企業の企業文化をどのように根付かせたいのかをよく話し合い、**共通認識を持ち**、その土台に立ってお互いの特殊性を理解し、かつ相手の持ちかけた提案をその特殊性の中でどのように適合させていくかといった方法論を話し合わなければなりません。

　手間のかかることですが、こうした土台からじっくりと共通の理解を構築していく作業が、国際環境でのビジネスではどうしても必要なのです。

　グローバル・スタンダードとは、共通の目的を認知し、その中でお互いの違いを認識し、そこからお互いの強い部分を抽出し、その強い部分をお互いの中で応用し、より強い結果を産み出すという、プロセスそのものを指すのです。単に自らの尺度を普遍化させることではないのだ、ということをよく心得ておきたいものです。

ソリューション

❶ アメリカ人は自分のやり方を押し付けるというステレオタイプ。実は日本人も海外に進出したとき同じように日本のやり方を通そうとやっきになる。お互いに蟹の横ばいにならないよう注意しよう。

❷ グローバル・スタンダードとは、自らの価値観を相手に押しつけることにあらず。お互いの特殊性を理解しながら、企業文化を伝達し、育てていく姿勢を維持しよう。

❸ 知っておこう、日本の常識は、違うビジネス文化の中では非常識。そして彼らの常識は日本では非常識となりうることを。自らの尺度を離れて世界の尺度を持とうではないか。

Here I would just like to consider what exactly is entailed in the words "global standards." Surely, rather than a setting up of standards that apply all across the board regardless of the actual conditions in various countries, what is needed is negotiation about the kind of business each company wants to develop in the world, and how best to let the corporate culture of each country take root—a **mutual recognition** of each other. An understanding on this kind of basis of each other's uniqueness will allow people to look for methods of adaptation of each other's proposals making allowances for that uniqueness.

It may be a time-consuming way of going about things, but the endeavor to build up solid and thoroughgoing mutual understanding on this kind of basis is absolutely necessary in business in a truly global marketplace.

"Global standards" speaks to a "process"—one in which all parties involved know about each other's objectives, and have a clear recognition of each other's differences. Then they can draw out each other's strong points, and apply those strong points in a way that is mutually beneficial and will give rise to even better results. I would like people to understand that applying global standards is not simply a matter of applying one's own standards in a universal way.

Solution

❶ There is a stereotype that Americans force their own ways of doing things on others. The truth is that when Japanese companies expanded overseas, they did the same thing. Be careful not to become like crabs that can only crawl sideways to each other.

❷ Global standards does not mean forcing people to follow your own values. It is important to understand each other's special characteristics, tell your partners about your corporate culture, and then build up a common one.

❸ Know that what is common sense in Japan can be seen as lacking in common sense in other countries' business cultures. And that what is common sense in other countries can be seen as lacking in common sense in Japan. Think about moving away from your own standards and adopting global ones.

事例

28

頑張ってシナジーを構築しよう!!

> お互いに本気なんだよ。そう、お互いに心からこの会社を、このビジネスを伸ばしたいと思っている。でもどうして、それがうまくいかないのか? そこが問題なんだ。

外国人の不満 誤解しないでください。私たちは、けっして日本人に我々の考え方を押しつけようとか、我々のやりかたがただ1つの方法だなどとは思っていないんです。ましてや、適当に日本の会社で働いて、うまく権利だけを主張して儲けてやろうとも思っていない。

おそらく、一部にはそんな不心得な連中もいるかもしれません。でも、悪い考えを持った人は世界中どこにでもいる。それは不幸なことです。でも、我々のほとんどは、心から仕事を通して日本の同僚やパートナーと一緒にビジネスを成功させたいと思っている。

それなのに、どうして仕事をはじめると、お互いにぎくしゃくして、**誤解が誤解を生み**、不幸な結果になってしまうのかがわからないんです。そのことが悲しいんです。時には、我々は霧の深い海の中に置き去りにされてしまったような不安を抱いてしまいます。

きっと日本人も同じように思っているんじゃないでしょうか。なぜうまくやって行けないのか? 同じ人間なのにどうしてなんでしょう?

Create synergy by working together!

> We're both sides committed; we all sincerely want to expand this company. But the problem is, somehow things go wrong.

Foreigner's grievance: Don't misunderstand us. We truly don't intend to force our way of thought on the Japanese; neither do we think our methods are the only ones. And still less do we believe that we can earn big bucks out of a Japanese company by putting in just an adequate amount of work and stressing our "rights" according to when it suits us.

Maybe there are some like that among us, but there are people with bad intentions all over the world. This is unfortunate. But most of us really do want to make a success out of our business through working on an equal footing with our Japanese partners.

So why, when we start the work, do we encounter such problems? Why do **misunderstandings give rise to further misunderstandings**, and it all ends so unhappily? We just don't understand it. It's truly troubling. Sometimes it really worries us; it feels like we've been abandoned at the bottom of the sea, in a deep fog.

I'm sure the Japanese must feel the same way. Why can't we get things to go right? We're all human beings—so why?

日本人の反論　私たちは、決して不可解な人間ではないんです。同じように笑ったり悲しんだり、興奮したり、がっかりしたりしてるじゃないですか。それなのに、外国人からすぐにステレオタイプにみられ、敬遠されてしまう。

　確かに、日本人の中には、日本文化だけに固執して、偏狭な考えにこりかたまっている人もいるでしょう。でも、そんな人、アメリカにだって、オーストラリアにだって、世界中どこにでもいるでしょう。こうした一部の印象だけを先走らせて、日本人は閉鎖的で不可解な人間だというふうに一般化しないでほしいんです。

　我々だって、あなたがたと一緒に仕事をして、同じ目標に取り組んで、日本のマーケットに少しでも多く海外の商品を紹介したいと思ってるし、海外に日本の技術で貢献したいんです。ただ、悩んでいるのは、海外の人とのコミュニケーションが思ったより難しいということなんです。

　こちらが善意でやっても逆にとられてしまったり、時には厳しく糾弾されたりで戸惑っています。どうすればいいのでしょう? 同じ人間なのにどうしてなんでしょう?

分析

　善意をもって、仕事に取り組もうと思っているのに、お互いに仕事をすればするほどぎくしゃくしてくる。これは、異文化の中でビジネスをしていくときに必ず乗り越えなければならない試練なのです。

　外国人も、日本人も、同じ人間なのにどうしてと溜息をついています。そう。どちらも人間として、善意をもってお互いによりよい結果を産み出そうと取り組んでいるのです。そのことはお互

Japanese retort: We're not hard to understand as human beings. We laugh, we cry, we get angry, or disappointed—in the same way as they do. So why are we always seen in a way that stereotypes or mocks us?

Certainly there are some amongst us who cling only to Japanese ways, or who hang on to narrow-minded ways of thinking. But you get that type of person in the States and Australia, and all over the world, in fact. I wish they wouldn't judge everyone by the impression given by this small segment of the population, and generalize that all Japanese are close-minded or incomprehensible.

No less than you do, we want to work together, toward the same goals, to try to introduce as many of your products as possible to the Japanese markets, and to contribute Japanese technology abroad. What bothers us, though, is that communication with people abroad seems to present more problems than we thought.

When we do things with **good intentions**, we get misunderstood, and occasionally we get denounced in a way that leaves us utterly confused. We want to do something about it—but what? How can human beings be so at odds?

Analysis

Despite the good intentions with which you set out to work together, when you start work, things get **out of joint** and don't go well. This is something you're always going to come up against and that you're going to have to get over when you do business with a foreign country.

Each side sighs and wonders how things could possibly get so difficult. After all, you say, we're "all human beings." Yes, both sides are made up of human beings, and each has the best intention—you want to work together so that you can produce better results. It's as well for

いに知っておく必要があるでしょう。

　でも、同じ人間じゃないかといって相手の不可解な対応に戸惑うのはいただけません。それは、同じ人間なのにと思って不満を抱いた瞬間に、自らの文化背景に基づく尺度を相手に押しつけて判断していることになるからです。

　相手には、こちらには知り得ない文化背景、社会環境によって培われた尺度があるのです。自らは決して万物の尺度ではないのです。相手の文化背景とそれに起因する行動や表現方法に対して理解をもつことから、全てははじまるべきでしょう。

　ビジネスでのコミュニケーションは、待ったなしの緊張した実践の場であればあるほど、尺度の違いが際だって現れ、それが誤解や不信感の原因となるのです。

　グローバルな環境で仕事をするとき、**巨視的には**、海外の人々とよりよきパートナーシップを築き上げるよう、組織造りに励まなければなりません。しかし、そうした組織造りのプロセスの一つ一つで、ここで触れた日々のコミュニケーションの壁を乗り越えるよう、お互いに努力していかなければならないことは、いうまでもないことです。

　各論での、コミュニケーションの問題を前向きに話し合い、信頼関係を培っていくことこそ、最も大切な業務の一つとなるのです。そうすれば、その企業は、**単一文化**だけでは決して思いつくこともない、創造性のあるアイデアや知恵、そして経験を世界中から集め、育てることのできる、強い組織として成長を遂げられるのです。そう、それが世界で仕事をすることの楽しさでもあり、生き甲斐でもあるのです。

both sides to be aware of that about each other.

But getting confused about the incomprehensible reactions of the other, just because you are "all human beings," is not quite enough. In the instant that you get irritated and think to yourself, "Surely we both act and feel the same way. We're both human beings," you are unfairly using your own culture's yardstick to measure the other person.

You've got to remember, the person has his or her own yardstick, which has behind it a cultural background and social environment that you can only attempt to get to know the whole of. Things will only start to go well when we show respect for other people's cultural backgrounds and for the actions and methods of expression that arise from them.

As far as communication in business is concerned, the differences in yardsticks tend to get more noticeable the more a situation is of the "last call" variety, filled with tension and urgency. This is what gives rise to misunderstanding and distrust.

When you work in a global environment, **macroscopically**, you've got to use a lot of energy to develop organizational set-ups that allow you to build even better partnerships with people in other countries. But it goes without saying that both sides have to put their very best efforts into getting over the kinds of barriers that I have indicated exist at each and every stage in the process of consolidating the infrastructure.

One of the most important parts of your duties involves establishing a trusting relationship, and talking with each other in a constructive way about your problems in communication in the discussion of every problem you encounter. If you can do this, your company will be able to truly evolve into a powerful entity, able to gather ideas with originality, and gain knowledge and experience from all over the world, in a way that would never have been possible had the company remained **mono-cultural**.

ソリューション

❶ お互いに善意をもって仕事しているのだ。ビジネスを発展させたいのだ。でも異文化の罠にかかればお互いを誤解し、相手をネガティブに捉えがち。そのプロセスとリスクを常に心において、ビジネスに取り組もう。

❷ 異文化では、お互いの強いところが合致すれば強力なシナジーが醸成される。多様な社会の多様な価値観を楽しめてこそ、真の国際人となるのだ。

❸ ビジネス上での異文化間の理解は1度では深まらない。何度も波を乗り越えるうちに、よいチームができてくる。面倒がらず、チェックポイントを設定し、建設的に、未来志向で、そして常に話し合い、聞き合うスタンスを保っていこう。

Solution

❶ People do business with good intentions toward one another. We want to develop our businesses, but it is easy to misunderstand each other and tend to perceive partners negatively by falling into the trap of cultural differences. Always be aware of that process and risk when doing business.

❷ Cultural differences can create a synergy through merging each other's strengths. By appreciating the various values of various societies, you will become truly international.

❸ You cannot gain a deep understanding of cultural differences in business all at once. A good team is built by repeatedly overcoming difficult situations. Establish checkpoints, be constructive, future oriented, and always take the approach of talking things over and listening to others, all without thinking of it as a nuisance.

English Conversational Ability Test
国際英語会話能力検定

● E-CATとは…

英語が話せるようになるための
テストです。インターネット
ベースで、30分であなたの発
話力をチェックします。

www.ecatexam.com

● iTEP®とは…

世界各国の企業、政府機関、アメリカの大学
300校以上が、英語能力判定テストとして採用。
オンラインによる90分のテストで文法、リー
ディング、リスニング、ライティング、スピー
キングの5技能をスコア化。iTEP®は、留学、就
職、海外赴任などに必要な、世界に通用する英
語力を総合的に評価する画期的なテストです。

www.itepexamjapan.com

言い返さない日本人［新装版］
海外との究極のコミュニケーション術

2021年8月2日 第1刷発行

著 者 山久瀬 洋二

発行者 浦 晋 亮

発行所 IBCパブリッシング株式会社
〒162-0804 東京都新宿区中里町29番3号 菱秀神楽坂ビル9F
Tel. 03-3513-4511 Fax. 03-3513-4512
www.ibcpub.co.jp

印刷所 株式会社シナノパブリッシングプレス

ISBN978-4-7946-0668-6